TRACING YOUR CHURCH OF ENGLAND ANCESTORS

A Guide for Family and Local Historians

Stuart A. Raymond

Pen & Sword

First published in Great Britain in 2017
PEN & SWORD FAMILY HISTORY
an imprint of
Pen & Sword Books Ltd
47 Church Street
Barnsley
South Yorkshire
S70 2AS

ISBN 978 1 47389 064 0

A CIP catalogue record for this book is
available from the British Library.

Typeset in Palatino and Optima by CHIC GRAPHICS

Printed and bound in England by
CPI Group (UK), Croydon, CR0 4YY

Pen & Sword Books Ltd incorporates the imprints of Pen & Sword
Archaeology, Atlas, Aviation, Battleground, Discovery, Family History,
History, Maritime, Military, Naval, Politics, Railways, Select, Social History,
Transport, True Crime, Claymore Press, Frontline Books, Leo Cooper,
Praetorian Press, Remember When, Seaforth Publishing and Wharncliffe.

For a complete list of Pen & Sword titles please contact
PEN & SWORD BOOKS LTD
47 Church Street, Barnsley, South Yorkshire, S70 2AS, England
E-mail: enquiries@pen-and-sword.co.uk
Website: www.pen-and-sword.co.uk

Contents

Chapter 10: Tracing Anglican Clergy   174
    A. Introduction: The Clergy of the Church of England
       Database   174
    B. Clerical Education   174
    C. The Clergy Career Path   177
    D. Clergy Subscription and Oaths   183
    E. Clerical Taxation   183
    F. Queen Anne's Bounty   185
    G. Deans and Canons   185
    H. The Civil War and Interregnum   186
    I. Biographical Works   188
    J. Armed Forces Chaplains   192
    K. Chaplains of Royal and Aristocratic Households   192
    L. Clergymen Overseas   192

Chapter 11: Other Sources   197
    A. Charles Booth's Interviews   197
    B. Diaries   197
    C. Commonwealth and Interregnum Records,
       1642–1660   199
    D. The Compton Census 1676   200
    E. The Ecclesiastical Census 1851   200
    F. Glynne's Church Notes   201
    G. Newspapers   201
    H. *Notitia Parochialis*   203
    I. Queen Anne Churches   204
    J. School Records   204
    K. Sermons   207

Notes   208
Place Name Index   219
Personal Index   221
Subject Index   222

ACKNOWLEDGEMENTS

My major debt in writing this book is to the authors whose works I have cited. I would also like to thank Marjorie for occasionally dragging me away from the computer. I am grateful to the librarians of Trowbridge, Sarum College and the Bodleian Library for their assistance. Simon Fowler, and one of my former Pharos students, have both made useful comments and saved me from errors. Any that remain are my responsibility, and I would be grateful if they could be brought to my attention.

Stuart A. Raymond

INTRODUCTION

Until the late seventeenth century, every English man and woman was a member of the Church of England. Legally, that continued to be the case for several centuries, although in practice Non-conformists and Roman Catholics denied their membership. Anglican priests, even today, recognize that they have an obligation to serve everyone in their parishes. It follows that everyone with English ancestors, at least in the nineteenth century and earlier, can claim Anglican ancestors.

This book explains how to trace Anglican ancestors. It is hoped that local historians will also find it useful. The documentary needs of the latter are very similar to those of the family historian, but are sometimes somewhat wider. Here, we are primarily concerned with records created within dioceses and parishes, although other records are mentioned where appropriate. Readers are assumed to have a basic knowledge of major sources, such as the civil registers of births, marriages and deaths, and the census returns. Two other basic sources – parish registers of baptisms, marriages and burials, and probate records – are actually records created by the Church of England, so are discussed here. The Church of England, incidentally, was the established church of England and Wales, and also of Ireland, but not of Scotland. The records of both Scotland and Ireland are not within the scope of this book.

We begin by placing the records that we need to consult in the context of the institution which created them. Chapter 1 provides a very brief outline of the history of Anglicanism. Chapter 2 describes the structure of the church, how clergy and laity operate within it, and why the records that we use were created. Some preliminaries to research are discussed in Chapter 3. The following chapters describe the various different sources that we need to consult in order to trace family and local history. Chapter 10 is solely devoted to the task of tracing clergymen, whose careers can frequently be traced in much more detail than is possible for most of the laity.

There are many terms used in this book which are peculiar to the Church of England. This jargon is generally explained when it is first mentioned. However, for a brief overview, see:

- Church Jargon
  www.churchsociety.org/issues_new/churchlocal/iss_church local_jargon.asp

The aim of this book is to suggest which sources might tell you something about your parish or your ancestors. As you read it, make a note of the various sources which might reveal some information about specific ancestors and follow them up either online or in a record office. Happy hunting!

Chapter 1

THE HISTORY OF THE CHURCH OF ENGLAND

After the crucifixion of Jesus, the message of the Gospel spread throughout the world. Discounting the myth that Joseph of Arimathea visited Glastonbury, it took perhaps two or three hundred years before it reached the island of Britain. The Church of England traces its ancestry back to two sources. The Celtic church flourished for several centuries before the Anglo-Saxon invasion. When Augustine was sent from Rome to evangelize the Anglo-Saxons in 697, he found that Celtic Christians were still active in the North and West, and were conducting their own missions in places like Lindisfarne and Iona.

Roman Catholic and Celtic traditions were different. It took half a century to meld them together. By the latter half of the eighth century, however, they had formed a unified body. The Church of England was not to be divided by doctrinal controversy again until the ideas of John Wycliffe prompted the Lollard 'heresy' to break out at the end of the fourteenth century.

Lollardy was uncharacteristic, and was quickly repressed, although it is possible that remnants survived to see some Wycliffite teachings adopted by early sixteenth-century Continental reformers, such as Martin Luther and John Calvin. Generally, however, early Tudor Englishmen were firmly attached to the Church of Rome. That attachment was strengthened by the imminence of death, which, in an age without modern medicine, was a constant threat. So was Hell. The great paintings of doom which could be seen over the chancel arch in many parish churches, one of which is still viewable

St Michael slaying the dragon at Ranworth in Norfolk.

at St. Thomas's church in Salisbury, illustrated what was thought to happen after death. God was depicted sitting in judgement. Demons stood ready to seize the damned, and cast them down into Hell, which was graphically portrayed as the gaping mouth of a monster. On the other hand, angels stood ready to escort those saved by the blood of Christ into Heaven. Salvation depended on the sacrifice of Christ, mediated through the church, the body of Christ. The church offered consolation in death, a means to shorten the time to be spent in Purgatory, and a gateway to eternal life.

Englishmen exercised a vibrant faith in the goodness of God, and in the power of the Resurrection. Their faith was expressed through the church, and through its services. The evidence of that faith is still all around us in the English landscape. It can be seen by anyone who cares to walk more than a mile or two in the English countryside: the landscape is full of fifteenth- and sixteenth-century church towers, which are rarely more than three or four miles apart. A lot of time, money, and effort went into their construction.

Protestants, however, thought that the Roman Church was full of abuses, notably the sale of indulgences, and the growth of the chantry system, both of which were claimed to reduce the time to be spent in Purgatory. They insisted that the reverence paid to

The twelfth-century chancel at St Levan in Cornwall, still used for worship today.

The fifteenth-century tower of Steeple Ashton in Wiltshire. Its steeple was destroyed by lightning.

Much of the church at Magor in Monmouthshire was rebuilt in the fifteenth century. Its churchyard is still in use.

The medieval rood screen at Ashton in Devon. It escaped destruction by sixteenth-century iconoclasts.

images was idolatrous, and argued that the Bible alone was the guide to faith.

It is unlikely that Protestantism would have made much headway in England had it not been for Henry VIII's determination to obtain a divorce from Katherine of Aragon at all costs. He convinced himself that the authority of the Pope over divorce proceedings was unjustified, withdrew the country from Papal obedience, and in 1534 had himself named supreme head of the Church of England by Act of Parliament. The royal arms began to appear in English churches, signifying the royal headship – or, in the view of one critic, the 'abomination of desolation' spoken of by the prophet Daniel.[1] Henry, nevertheless, remained a convinced conservative in other religious matters, and refused to allow the changes in doctrine which Protestants advocated. But when it came to money, he was all for seizing as much of it from the church as he could. That allowed Protestantism to creep in. Some redundant monasteries had recently been closed down by Cardinal Wolsey, whose servant Thomas Cromwell had overseen much of the administration of closure. When Wolsey failed to obtain a divorce for his master, he was dismissed – but his role as Henry's chief minister was taken by his servant. Cromwell also became 'vicegerent', giving him more power over the church than any other layman before or since, and vitiating Henry's religious conservatism. He used his administrative experience to carry out a wholesale dissolution of the monasteries, which he justified to Henry on the grounds that the Crown benefited immensely from the seizure of their lands. He would have been reluctant to mention to Henry that the dissolution also destroyed a major prop of conservative doctrine – although in 1536 the Northern rebels of the Pilgrimage of Grace were keen to point it out to him.

It was not the Pilgrims who destroyed Cromwell. Rather, it was simply that Henry did not like the Queen that Cromwell found for him in Flanders, and that courtiers who did not like Cromwell persuaded the King to oust him. The vicegerent suffered decapitation in consequence, but not before he had ordered the placement of an English bible in every parish church, and created the conditions in which Thomas Cranmer, who had been made Archbishop of Canterbury at Henry's instigation, could orchestrate a full-scale introduction of Protestantism into England.

The death of Henry VIII, and the accession of his son, Edward VI, changed everything. Edward had been brought up under Protestant tuition, and had absorbed the faith of his tutors. Although he was only a child, he encouraged the Protestant reformation to take root in his kingdom. Prayers for the dead were out, so the numerous chantries which had been established to conduct them were dissolved. Prayers to saints were also out, so the iconoclasts had a field day destroying their images, and, in the process, destroying most of the artwork of medieval England. Wall paintings in churches were whitewashed, or replaced with Biblical texts. Rood lofts were destroyed, and the stairs to them blocked up.

Blocked-off stairs to the rood loft at St Buryan in Cornwall, evidence of the zeal of sixteenth-century reformers in this remote parish.

The doctrine of transubstantiation, which argued that the bread and wine offered in the Eucharist became, in reality, the body and blood of Christ, was also discarded. Consequently, altars for sacrifice were no longer needed, and were replaced with a table in the nave. Processions ceased. The sermon became the focus of church services – if preachers could be found. And, in 1549, the *Book of Common Prayer* was introduced. That caused another rebellion, this time in

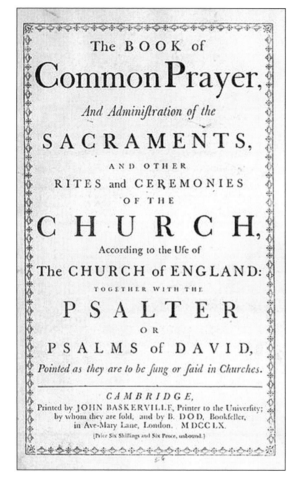

The Book of Common Prayer *is still in print after almost 500 years of use. This is a 1760 edition.*

Devon and Cornwall. Again, the rebellion was quashed. But the rebels' aims were achieved a couple of years later, when Edward VI died, and Mary I succeeded to the throne.

Mary claimed to be a devout Catholic. She reversed all that Cranmer had done, had him burnt, and appointed Cardinal Pole to succeed him as Archbishop of Canterbury. Protestants who did not want to suffer Cranmer's fate fled to the Continent, many to Calvin's Geneva. Mary experienced little opposition to the reintroduction of the old religion. It had been vibrant before Henry's divorce proceedings; most Englishmen wanted to see its vibrancy continue, and to bring back traditional forms of worship. The Queen, however, had insufficient time to place the old church back onto a firm foundation. Only a handful of monasteries were re-established. She could not persuade gentlemen who had purchased monastic lands to disgorge them. It was a difficulty that Mary was unable to solve before she died in 1558. Her failure to re-instate Roman Catholicism was due to the brevity of her reign, and to the fact that she was succeeded by her half-sister, the Protestant Elizabeth.

Elizabeth's primary task was to establish her authority in church and state. Her Protestantism was of a very conservative character; for example, she regarded married clergy with great suspicion.[2] She clashed with the radical Calvinist exiles flocking back to England from Geneva.[3] Few of them shared her views, yet they were the only people available to staff the upper echelons of her Church. Marian bishops refused to cooperate with her, and were ousted, leaving the Queen with the difficult task of reconciling radical Calvinist bishops with her predominantly Catholic subjects. She sought a *via media* between the two positions, and won the respect of both, even though she had to suspend one Archbishop in the process.[4]

The Elizabethan settlement is still the basis of the Church of England. Archbishop Cranmer created a liturgy which depends on congregations listening and responding. The cadences of his prayers have continued to ring out at matins and evensong. Since Elizabeth's reign, almost every generation of Englishmen and women have responded to the words 'Oh Lord, open thou our lips' with the reply 'And our mouths shall shew forth thy praise'. And again, the words 'O God, make speed to save us', have brought forth the response 'O Lord, make haste to help us'. The recitation of the liturgy has continued to be the prime feature of Anglican worship, although the pattern of services has been modified over the centuries – for example, by the introduction of hymns. It is, however, only in the generation of the present writer that the use of Cranmer's *Book of Common Prayer* has gradually diminished.

Bishop Jewell, the sixteenth-century Calvinist reformer, is reputed to have preached from this pulpit at Monkton Farleigh in Wiltshire.

The success of the 1559 settlement was partially due to Elizabeth's good sense in knowing what her subjects would accept, and to her refusal to 'open windows into men's souls'. But it was perhaps primarily due to her longevity. By the time she died, in 1603, most of her subjects had no memory of anything other than the *Prayer Book* service. They did, however, know full well the extent of Roman Catholic hostility to their country, as exemplified by the 1570 Papal excommunication of Elizabeth I, and the 1588 Spanish Armada. They also knew, or, at least, thought they knew, the horrors that 'Bloody Mary' had inflicted on their Protestant ancestors, graphically if somewhat tendentiously described by Foxe's popular *Book of Martyrs* (also known as the *Acts and Monuments*).[5] The introduction of a new translation of the Bible, the Authorised Version, in 1611 marked the point at which England had become, irreversibly, a Protestant country.

Elizabethan uniformity was to be challenged. Charles I did not possess Elizabeth's good sense, and did not understand why many

Archbishop Thomas Cranmer, author of the Book of Common Prayer.

Puritans were prepared to take up arms to defend their beliefs. Although the issue when civil war broke out in 1642 was control of the militia, the religious issues quickly surfaced in Parliamentary deliberations. The emphasis Archbishop Laud placed on sacramental worship, downgrading the importance of sermons, bringing back altars and railing them in, was seen as Romanizing. Whilst Laud claimed to be campaigning for the 'beauty of holiness' in Church of England services, his opponents saw the ceremonial that he sought to introduce as the thin end of the Roman wedge.

Laudian extremism in one direction led to Puritan extremism in the other direction. The Pilgrim Fathers crossed the Atlantic Ocean to escape persecution, and to worship in a pure church. When Parliament had the power to do so, it abolished bishops, and sought to bring English ecclesiastical polity more into conformance with the Geneva model. Parliament, however, was sharply divided. Those who sought the establishment of a strict Presbyterian system of church governance were not sufficiently strong to overcome the resistance of the Independents, who argued for the autonomy of individual congregations. Whilst they argued, many other sects arose, amongst them Fifth Monarchy men, Muggletonians, Ranters, Quakers and Baptists. And the term 'Anglican' had to be invented[6] for those who claimed to follow traditional Church of England practices.

Their claim was dubious. Before the Civil War, Puritans had as good a claim to be Anglicans as the high church Laudians, if not better. The term 'orthodox', to the Elizabethan churchman, meant Calvinist.[7] It was only under Charles I that the Calvinistic doctrine of predestination (the doctrine that God predestined men to be saved before they were born) began to be questioned, and only after the Restoration that Arminianism, its denial, began to be widely accepted.

The Laudians seemed to recover their position at the Restoration, although Parliament made it quite clear that it, rather than the bishops, had the final say in ecclesiastical matters. Royalist clergy ejected during the Interregnum returned to their benefices, and intruders were themselves ejected. New bishops were appointed; deans and chapters returned to their Cathedrals; the church courts were restored. Sects such as the Ranters and the Fifth Monarchy Men disappeared.

Despite these developments, the Church of England was never again the church of the whole nation. Despite Charles II's promise of toleration, almost 2,000 clergy who refused to conform to the restored church were ejected from their livings in 1662. Most, like Richard Baxter, had wished to remain within the national church, but the Cavalier Parliament imposed such onerous requirements on them that they felt they could not conscientiously do so. They were required to disavow the Solemn League and Covenant, which many of them had sworn to. They had to declare publicly that they would strictly adhere to the *Book of Common Prayer*, which many of them had attacked in their sermons. And they had to affirm that it was illegal to take up arms against the Crown under any circumstances whatsoever.

The Cavalier Parliament knew what it was doing: it aimed to drive Puritanism out of existence. It would not permit the toleration promised by Charles II. His 1672 Declaration of Indulgence was countermanded by the 1673 Test Act,[8] which required all appointees to public office to take Anglican communion. Proof that they had done so was provided by sacrament certificates (see below, p.138). Similar opposition greeted James II's Declaration of Indulgence in 1687. That however, was quickly followed by William of

Richard Baxter, leader of the Nonconformists

Orange's invasion, and by the Dissenters' support for him. They were rewarded by suspension of the penal laws against them, although they remained excluded from public office, and from the universities.

Like the Presbyterians during the Interregnum, the Cavalier Parliament did not have the power to enforce its will. Its 1662 legislation had unintended consequences. Many ejected clergymen gathered congregations, and formed their own Nonconformist, or 'gathered', churches. At first, parochial clergy attempted to win dissenters over by persuasion, then by force. But many Nonconformists could not be persuaded. The story of early Nonconformity is told in the records of Quarter Sessions and the church courts.[9]

At first, the denominational loyalties of particular congregations were fluid, at least amongst Presbyterians, Independents and Baptists. These mainstream Nonconformist denominations frequently worked together. There was, however, little love lost between them and the more radical 'sectaries', such as the Quakers. The Quakers were the only denomination who were firmly united with each other, and totally opposed to the established church. They challenged the social structure by refusing to take oaths, to doff their hats to authority or to pay tithes (see below, pp.99–102). Consequently, their 'sufferings' were many – and were meticulously recorded by their Meetings in Quaker Books of Sufferings.[10] Their unity was essential for their survival.

Dissenters could not, however, prevent the post-Restoration church gaining the loyalty of the vast majority of the population. That was demonstrated by the substantial number of churchwardens' presentments (see below, pp.110–11) for failure to attend church made in the early years of the restored regime. Churchwardens were initially eager to support the restored bishops.[11] This support was largely support for the traditional liturgy, and for the regular observance of days such as Christmas, Easter and Good Friday. Despite the absence of the *Book of Common Prayer* in the 1650s,[12] most adults in 1660 had been brought up on it, and welcomed its re-introduction. It formed the basis of popular religion almost until our own days. Until the mid-eighteenth century, most people attended church regularly, and most churches were full.[13]

Overall, however, the Restoration settlement carried the seeds of decline. Clerical insistence on formal worship, their intolerance of dissent, and their failure to understand popular religion all boded ill for the future of the Church of England. Post-Restoration clergy tended to see any questioning of their authority as incipient separatism, and responded accordingly.

Although the church had been restored, no attention had been paid to the need to reform its archaic disciplinary procedures, its extremes of clerical income, its potential for excessive pluralism[14] and the diocesan geography which hindered effective episcopal oversight. All of these problems were recognized, but no action was taken.

Another problem arose when William III was crowned king. Many clergy refused to swear oaths recognizing his authority, since they had already sworn to uphold James II's authority. These 'non-jurors' included nine bishops (including Archbishop Sancroft) and some 400 clergy. They formed their own denomination, consecrated new bishops and survived almost until the end of the eighteenth century. More clergy joined them on the accession of George I in 1714.[15]

Other issues arose during the eighteenth century. The growing wealth of the clergy, their elitist education and the fact that a substantial number were the sons of clergy, gave the profession an increasing sense of caste. Clergymen in Elizabethan times had generally been worth a little less than yeomen. The seventeenth-century parsonage was still the house of a working farmer. Farming, however, was incompatible with gentility. As clerical wealth increased in the eighteenth century, so did the clergy's sense of social superiority. They ceased to farm, and imposed social distinctions between themselves and the people they were supposed to serve.

Many eighteenth-century incumbents had little sense of vocation, and little understanding of the faith. Archdeacon Prideaux condemned the 'excessive ignorance he had met with in such as offered themselves for ordination'.[16] It did not help that young ordinands had little or no training in either pastoral care or theology; instead, university gave them a gentleman's education in classics. Clerical diaries such as those of Parson Woodforde frequently reveal clergymen who seem to have been 'more concerned with the dinner menu than with the souls of their parishioners'.[17] Many candidates did what their fathers and their teachers told them to do, and became clergymen in order to fund their lives as gentlemen. Once inducted into a living, they could shelter behind their legal freehold and ignore their bishops, who had very limited sanction against clergy who neglected their duties. The clergy's dependence on tithes was another important issue. This occasionally led to disputes with the laity, making it difficult for clergy to provide the pastoral care which was their *raison d'être*. Nevertheless, the relationship between most clergy and their parishioners remained respectful, and agreement on the payment of tithes was usually possible without resort to the courts.[18]

The Church of England clung to its claim to be the *via media* between the extremes of Papalism and sectarianism. In 1700, the numbers of Nonconformists and Roman Catholics were small and diminishing.[19] Nonconformist numbers halved between 1660 and 1760 – a trend that was to be dramatically reversed in the following century.

Disputes within the Church died down in the eighteenth century; parties virtually disappeared until almost its end. The post-Restoration Church perhaps reached the height of its popularity in the first half of the century. But even then it was facing the challenge of Deism, that is, the rejection of revelation in favour of rationalism. In the second half, it faced the challenge of evangelicalism, which led to the rapid growth of Nonconformity towards the end of the century. These challenges were powerful reminders to the clergy that they needed to be united. Perhaps even more critical for the future of the church was the somewhat neglected challenge of ministering to the laity.

Whereas the authorities gave priority to ensuring that its ministers conformed to the 1662 Act of Uniformity, and to the liturgical requirements of its canons, the laity expected clergy to provide a high standard of pastoral care and to live unimpeachable lives. Services were to be conducted reverently, children were to be catechised, the sick were to be visited. It was the clergyman's duty to make himself available to his parishioners, and to conduct baptisms, churchings (the reception of mothers back into the church after giving birth), marriages, and funerals. They might be called upon to draw up wills. Many eighteenth-century clergymen actively promoted the education of the poor.[20] Much depended on the individual clergyman, and on his relationship with his parishioners. A popular man could persuade everyone to attend church. An unpopular minister could drive everyone away. Churchwardens' presentments include many complaints against ministers, and demonstrate the importance of the relationship between clergy and people. Scandalous or neglectful clergy could have serious consequences for the conduct of worship.

The persecution of Nonconformists and Roman Catholics after the Restoration was not welcomed by most people, and, despite their initial enthusiasm, churchwardens increasingly refused to present them at visitation. Similarly, parish constables were reluctant to present them at Quarter Sessions. The church courts gradually became ineffective. The penalties they could impose – penance and excommunication – lost their importance, especially when they were imposed on Nonconformists and Roman Catholics.[21] A 1703 judgement declared that disciplining the laity under the canons (ecclesiastical law) was illegal. In 1737 another judgement held that the canons could not be used for prosecution purposes unless they had been confirmed by Parliamentary statute.[22] Tithe disputes were increasingly heard by civil judges in the Westminster courts, rather than in Diocesan Consistory courts.

The inability of the Church of England to rapidly create new parishes (an Act of Parliament was required for each one), meant that the eighteenth-century Church of England was ill-placed to respond to the challenge of industrialization, urbanization and demographic growth: its resources were in the declining rural areas, not in the rapidly-expanding cities. Queen Anne's Bounty (see below, p.185) had considerable success in augmenting the incomes of the poorest incumbents. Between 1704 and 1830, the number of livings worth under £50 per annum was reduced from 3,800 to a mere 300.[23] Despite this success, however, major inadequacies still existed, and continued to exist for the ensuing century. In 1833, half of England's benefices either had an income of under £150 (widely regarded as the minimum necessary to support a clergyman), or lacked adequate accommodation, or had an incumbent who was not fit enough to run his parish.[24] When the Pluralities Acts of 1838 and 1850 deprived clergymen of the possibility of holding more than one benefice, clergy incomes gradually fell. When agricultural prices slumped in the 1880s, the tithe rent-charge granted to the clergy under the Tithe Commutation Act of 1836 also slumped. It has been argued that the clergy were only able to maintain their position because many of them had private incomes.

The Church of England was based on the parish. Each priest was responsible for his own patch, and for whatever religious activity was conducted on it. John Wesley claimed that the world was his parish, but the claim provided a fundamental challenge to the structure of the Church of England and attracted the ire of many parish priests. Opposition to itinerancy meant opposition to the Methodist revival. Evangelicalism's impact on the Church of England, at first, was negative. Wesleyan methods were profoundly distrusted by most Anglican ministers. They were too reminiscent of the 'enthusiasm' shown by Interregnum sectaries, who were thought to have almost destroyed the Church of England. Many clergy would have agreed with the attitude of the pseudonymous Peter Paragraph:

> Cromwell like you did first pretend
> Religion was his only end
> But soon the mask away did fling
> Pull'd down the church and killed the King[25]

18

John Wesley at Epworth Old Rectory.

Despite the fact that John Wesley himself remained an Anglican minister until his dying day, his societies were shunned by the Church of England hierarchy. Eventually, like the ejected ministers of 1662, they were forced to form themselves into a separate denomination. The refusal of most eighteenth-century Anglican clergy to engage with the evangelical revival meant that many deserted them, looking elsewhere for spiritual nourishment.

Nevertheless, there was no coordinated episcopal response to the Methodist challenge. And a spark of evangelicalism had been planted within the established church. It burst into life at the end of the eighteenth century. Richard Raikes' Sunday Schools, begun in Rochdale in 1780, William Wilberforce's campaign against the slave trade, Hannah More's support for the education of the poor, and the belief that Britain had a responsibility to promote Christianity in India all derived from evangelical faith. The Church Missionary Society (see below, pp.169–70), and the Religious Tract Society, were both founded in 1799. Evangelicals came together in the Clapham Sect[26] to promote their various causes.

The Clapham Sect played an important role in social reform.

Reform also came from Anglo-Catholics. Joshua Watson's Hackney Phalanx played a major role in creating societies concerned with promoting the education of the poor, supporting curates and building churches. The National Society for Promoting the Education of the Poor in the Principles of the Established Church founded innumerable schools, and became the voice of the church on educational matters throughout the nineteenth century. The Additional Curates Society provided grants to support curates in parishes which could not afford to do so. The Incorporated Church Building Society played a major role in financing the building of new churches.[27]

The Oxford Movement was also Anglo-Catholic.[28] Its aims were outlined in ninety *Tracts for the Times* (hence the name 'Tractarians').

The movement was perhaps more important for its approach to worship than for its work in society. It sprang to life opposing the reform of the Irish church, but quickly became a movement to centre Anglican worship in the sacrament of the Eucharist. It was naturally attacked for its Romanizing tendencies. Unlike the attacks of the Puritans on Laud, these attacks had some justification: several hundred Anglican clergy followed Newman when he defected to the Roman Catholics in 1845. Despite their defection, the Tractarians gave the clergy a new conception of their role in society. The clerical profession gradually ceased to be merely a means of providing careers for gentlemen's sons; instead, it became a vocation. Priests were increasingly seen as men set apart from secular society in order to provide spiritual leadership. Parishioners were encouraged to address them as 'Father'.

These evangelical and high church groups took very different approaches, but were united in seeking spiritual renewal. They all wanted to increase the clergy's pastoral effectiveness, to improve standards of preaching, and to strengthen clerical discipline. They invented Victorian respectability. And they gave Anglicans an increasing range of choices in their styles of churchmanship. The reforms of the nineteenth century took place against the backdrop of these movements for spiritual renewal.

Reform was badly needed. By 1800, industrialization and demographic growth meant that the parochial structure of the Church of England was severely hindering the Church's mission to the industrialized masses. Urban clergy could find themselves charged with the cure of thousands of souls. By contrast, most rural clergymen only had a few hundred souls in their charge, and had plenty of time to devote to scholarly pursuits, to the hunt, or to their magisterial duties. For many, pastoral visits were what happened when someone was dying. The relationship of many clergymen to their flocks was purely formal. That formality was one factor contributing to the disappearance of most labourers from the pews of rural churches during the nineteenth century.

In towns like Leeds and Liverpool, the labourers could not attend anyway. There were no seats for them. The parish of Leeds almost trebled in size between 1801 and 1841 from 53,000 to 152,000.[29] The St Marylebone district of London had only 8,700 seats in churches for 76,624 inhabitants.[30] The problem was not confined to major cities; in the Archdeaconry of Derby, only c.14 per cent of the seats were available for the poor in the mid-1820s.[31]

The working classes were being lost to the established church. The Hackney Phalanx saw that new churches were desperately needed, and founded the Incorporated Church Building Society in 1818. It raised £54,000 in its first year, supported the building of many new churches during the following century or so, and insisted that seats in them should be free. At the same time, a Parliamentary grant of £1,000,000 was made to establish the Church Building Commission. In 1824, a further grant of £500,000 was made. London alone gained thirty-eight new capacious, if utilitarian, 'Waterloo' churches.

There were no more Parliamentary grants. However, in 1833, Parliament finally took action to reform the antiquated structures of the Church of England. The new Ecclesiastical Commission (which absorbed the Church Building Commission in 1856) was given the task of reviewing the central administrative structures of the church. It recommended an extensive rearrangement of the dioceses, equalization of episcopal income and the diversion of money being spent on cathedral sinecures to improve pastoral care in the parishes. Some of its recommendations were carried through when it became permanent in 1836. Many cathedral canonries were suspended, and sinecures suppressed. The money saved was devoted to the augmentation of poor livings, the endowment of new churches and the employment of additional ministers. Diocesan reform, however, had to wait. The only new diocese created was Ripon. The Diocese of Bristol was abolished. Its two parts, Bristol and Dorset, were amalgamated with the Dioceses of Gloucester and Salisbury respectively. It was not until the 1870s and 1880s that a more thorough-going reform of diocesan boundaries was undertaken.[32]

Whilst the Church of England was reforming itself, Nonconformity, and especially Methodism, grew by leaps and bounds.[33] The English had more religious choice in the nineteenth century than ever before. The Church of England faced fierce competition. By the time of the 1851 religious census,[34] the numbers of Anglicans and Non-conformists attending church were almost equal: the Church of England had ceased to enjoy the loyalty of half of the worshipping population, and had, in the eyes of many, become merely another Christian denomination. Admittedly, many claimed allegiance to the established church, but never attended; McLeod suggests that 60 per cent of the population were Anglican.[35] Even worse, fewer than half of the population attended any church at all. Perhaps that was no great change, and the churches should have congratulated themselves on achieving such a high turnout. The issue was not a new one, although the ecclesiastical bench had been reluctant to admit it. The Bishop of Hereford was so dispirited at the numbers attending churches in his diocese in 1788 that he refused to record them. In 1800, in a small part of the Diocese of Lincoln, just one-third of the population attended.[36] Going further back, it is clear that attendance after the Restoration was not regarded as being satisfactory. Unfortunately, we have little other statistical evidence prior to 1851. What can be said, however, is that the working classes had not been entirely lost. Although church attendance in working-class parishes was low, nevertheless, perhaps 50 per cent of those attending church throughout the country were members of that class.[37]

The growth of Nonconformity was reflected in the increasing opposition to compulsory church rates. They had frequently replaced the old practice of raising funds from convivial gatherings, sometimes known as church ales, which had attracted Puritan ire. By the nineteenth century, church rates were meeting increasing opposition. They could only be levied with the consent of churchwardens and vestries. Nonconformists were entitled to vote in their election, and their increasing numbers meant that they were frequently able to outvote Anglicans. Church rates were abolished in 1868.

Despite Nonconformist growth, attempts to disestablish the Church of England failed. The Liberation Society was founded in 1844, and played an important role in the campaign against church rates. But, although the Church of Ireland and the Church of Wales were disestablished, in 1871 and 1920 respectively, the Society failed to achieve its ultimate objective. The Church of England is still the established church in England.

Nonconformity outpaced the Church of England, but, nevertheless, Anglicanism experienced impressive growth in the nineteenth century. It was encouraged by the new seriousness demanded by both the evangelicals and the tractarians. Clergy numbers expanded from 14,613 in 1841, to 24,968 in 1911. Some 1,500 new churches were built in the first half of the nineteenth century. Between 1840 and 1875 about 5,300 medieval parish churches were restored or rebuilt; the total number of Anglican churches increased by c.25 per cent. The new churches were frequently larger than their predecessors. Numbers consequently increased. There were 605,000 communicants on Easter Day in 1831, and 2,293,000 in 1911. At the beginning of the twentieth century, baptismal numbers as a percentage of the total population were increasing; in 1885 there were 62.3 per cent; by 1917 there were 70.5 per cent.[38] The growth rate was outpacing the growth rate of the English population as a whole. Anglicanism reclaimed some of its lost ground in the late nineteenth century.[39]

Nineteenth-century clergy were expected to be devout. Men like Walter Hook, rector of Leeds, set the tone. He, perhaps more than anyone else, established the pattern of the devoted and inexhaustible vicar, who was 'like an admiral commanding a squadron of curates in the battle for the city's soul'.[40] Between 1837 and 1859, he raised the money to build twenty-two new churches, twenty-three new vicarages and twenty-seven schools.

Growth was aided by music. Some Puritans had frowned on music, and the Elizabethan Convocation had once come within one vote of banning organs. But the singing of psalms became popular in the seventeenth century, and in the eighteenth century many rustic village bands provided music. At Coddenham (Suffolk), a pipe organ was installed in 1817 to assist the singing of psalms, and the vicar formed a children's choir.[41] Coddenham led the way. In subsequent decades many village bands were replaced with organs and choirs. The choir stalls in our churches date from the mid-nineteenth century. So does singing of the liturgy. Wesleyan hymns became popular, and were added to by such Anglican luminaries as Sabine Baring-Gould ('Onward Christian soldiers') and J.M. Neale ('The strife is o'er'). *Hymns Ancient and Modern*, inspired by the Oxford Movement, was introduced in 1861. The Royal College of Organists was founded in 1864. The *English Hymnal* was published

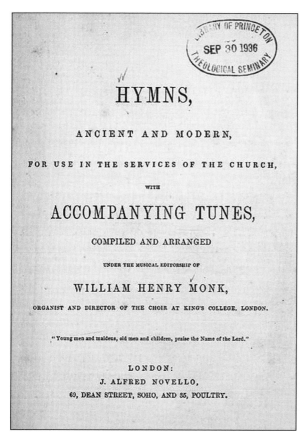

Hymns Ancient and Modern *has provided most of the hymns used in Anglican worship since it was first published in 1861.*

in 1906. In the 1890s, perhaps 2,000,000 hymnbooks were sold every year.[42] Although Methodist hymn singing was renowned, nevertheless, the re-invention of English church music in the nineteenth century was predominantly an Anglican affair.[43]

By 1900, the Victorians had vastly increased the number of churches. Parochial ministry had been revitalized, clergy numbers had increased dramatically and clergy education was providing a decent preparation for ministry. The resources of the church seemed to be employed to maximum effect. Many of those resources were being used for philanthropic purposes. In Lambeth at least, district visitors from the churches were continually looking for ways to help their neighbours, and were active in just about every street in the borough. The Victorian churches were arguable England's 'most important voluntary social institution'.[44] And a copy of the Bible could be found in almost every home. Many were used to record family trees.[45]

Despite all the clergy's effort, however, the church had to face new challenges at the beginning of the twentieth century. The horrors of the First World War led some to lose faith in the God of love.[46] However, it was not until the second half of the century that attendance at church began to seriously decline. This had many causes. Perhaps most importantly, the Welfare State increasingly provided many of the social services that the Victorian church had provided, making the church seem irrelevant, and depriving it of an important point of contact with society. The Victorian church perhaps expended so much energy on providing social services that it failed to recruit the committed membership needed to ensure that it continued to flourish in twentieth-century conditions. Many of those who actually attended church saw it merely as a 'public ritual of positive assent to a system of communal controls'; attendance was a matter of status in society, rather than of faith in God.[47]

Another problem was that the death rate at the end of the nineteenth century was in decline. Where there had been 25 deaths per annum for every 1,000 people in the mid-nineteenth century, by 1920 there were only 12. The Church could no longer place its emphasis on the importance of dying a good death, since death had largely been relegated to old age, and had ceased to be noticed by the younger generation in the way that it had been in previous centuries. Hell ceased to have relevance to young people, who had to be won for Christ by concentrating on this life. Nevertheless, it was still possible as late as 1944 to pass legislation requiring a daily corporate act of worship in every state-funded school. However, the removal of denominational involvement in religious education, and the lack of properly-trained catechists capable of teaching it adequately, meant that it became the least-favoured subject in the school curriculum. The fact that a third of children were enrolled in Sunday Schools in 1950 may have compensated for this problem in the early years – but enrolment steadily decreased, and by the late 1970s a mere 7 per cent of children were enrolled.[48] Part of the explanation for the ensuing decline in religious belief must lie in the fact that pupils in state schools during the 1950s and 1960s were not properly catechised.

The Church also experienced political interference. A liturgy that had been written in the sixteenth century was felt to be no longer suitable for use in the twentieth century. High churchmen felt that the *Book of Common Prayer* was liturgically inadequate. It was true that the language needed to be brought up to date. Indeed, Cranmer's original preface to the *Book of Common Prayer* had stated that it was written 'in such a language and ordre as is moste easy and plain for the understandying'. That had ceased to be true by the twentieth century, and the language was off-putting for some of the laity. But the primary motive for revision was to provide for a more sacramental and Catholic approach to Anglican worship. A new liturgy was approved by the Church Assembly, and presented for Parliamentary approval in 1928. It was rejected – twice! Nevertheless, the book was printed, and used by many clergy.

The second half of the twentieth century saw dramatic falls in church attendance and membership. Numbers had remained steady during the first half of the twentieth century, but after the Second World War they began to fall. In 1940, 3,388,859 members were counted. By 1970, the number had fallen to 2,558,966. In 1990, there were a mere 1,290,500.[49] The falling numbers were reflected in the closure of about a tenth of the existing church buildings since 1860. There have been many fewer new buildings, most of which are smaller than their predecessors.[50] There has, however, been much revision of the liturgy, including the late twentieth-century re-introduction of the *Pax* – the sharing of the peace – in communion, after over four centuries of its absence.

After the Second World War, the *Book of Common Prayer* was considered to be hindering the work of the Church. The Church Assembly moved cautiously, and persuaded a Parliament which had largely lost interest in church affairs to authorize the *Alternative Service Book* in 1980, for use alongside Cranmer's work. Liturgical reform has not, however, stopped there. The new book was replaced by *Common Worship* in 2000. And many Anglicans have ceased to use set liturgies, or have heavily adapted them for their own situations. The idea that uniformity of worship is important has lost much of its support.

The church was also prepared to take a fresh look at its role in the most deprived areas of the inner cities. The 1980s report *Faith in the City* provided direction for the work of the Church in those areas, and demonstrated that, almost at the end of the twentieth century, it still retained the ability to make a real difference to people's lives in the worst situations – and to upset the government. By the end of the twentieth century, the Church of England was a large, vigorous denomination, whose worshippers were attracted by its sacramental commitment. It still had much residual support from non-church-goers, evidenced by the baptisms, marriages, and funerals it conducted for them. But it had ceased to be regarded as anything more than just a denomination. That failure probably had a great deal to do with the fact that, until the early twentieth century, the Church was an institution governed by the conventions of social class.

FURTHER READING

There are far too many works on Church of England history to provide a comprehensive listing here. Those that are noted below are merely those that I have found useful in preparing this book. Two useful handbooks may be mentioned first:

- Buchanan, Colin. *Historical Dictionary of Anglicanism*. (Rowman & Littlefield, 2015).
- Friar, Stephen. *The Companion to Churches*. (History Press, 2011).

The nature of the Church of England is such that most historians tell its story by recounting the history of the church in England: the history of the denomination is the major component of most books on that topic:

- Edwards, David L. *Christian England*. (Rev ed. Fount Paperbacks, 1989).
- Moorman, J.R.H. *A History of the Church in England*. (2nd ed. Adam & Charles Black, 1967).
- Rosman, Doreen. *The Evolution of the English Churches*. (Cambridge University Press, 2003).

An interesting collection of essays is found in:

- Gilley, Sheridan, and Sheils, W.J., eds. *A History of Religion in Britain: Practice and Belief from Pre-Roman Times to the Present*. (Blackwell, 1994).

There are numerous histories of particular periods, and especially of the Reformation. On the transition from Roman Catholicism, the authority is now:

- Duffy, Eamon. *The Stripping of the Altars: Traditional Religion in England 1400-1580*. (2nd ed. Yale University Press, 1992).

See also:

- Cross, Claire. *Church and People: England 1450-1660*. (2nd ed. Blackwell, 1999).

For the Elizabethan and Stuart church, see:

- Collinson, Patrick. *The Religion of Protestants: the Church in English Society, 1559-1625*. (Clarendon Press, 1982).
- Maltby, Judith. *Prayer Book and People in Elizabethan and Stuart England*. (Cambridge University Press, 1998). This includes brief studies of a number of Cheshire parishes.

The late seventeenth-century church is the subject of:

- Spurr, John. *The Restoration Church of England 1646-1689*. (Yale University Press, 1991).

There are several works on the long eighteenth century:

- Jacob, W.M. *Lay People and Religion in the Early Eighteenth Century*. (Cambridge University Press, 1996).
- Sykes, Norman. *From Sheldon to Secker: Aspects of English Church History, 1660-1768*. (Cambridge University Press, 1959).
- Virgin, Peter. *The Church in an Age of Negligence: ecclesiastical structure and problems of church reform, 1700-1840*. (James Clarke & Co., 1989).
- Walsh, John, Haydon, Colin, and Taylor, Stephen, eds. *The Church of England c.1689-c.1833: from Toleration to Tractarianism*. (Cambridge University Press, 1993).

For the nineteenth century, see:

- Chadwick, Owen. *The Victorian Church*. (2nd ed. 2 vols. Adam & Charles Black, 1970–2).

- Knight, Frances. *The Nineteenth-Century Church and English Society*. (Cambridge University Press, 1995).
- Cox, Jeffrey. *The English Churches in a Secular Society: Lambeth, 1870-1930*. (Oxford University Press, 1982).

Twentieth-century history is covered by:

- Hastings, Adrian. *A History of English Christianity 1920-1990*. (3rd ed. SCM Press, 1991).
- Robbins, Keith. *England, Ireland, Scotland, Wales: the Christian Church, 1900-2000*. (Oxford University Press, 2008).

An introduction to the local church and its community is provided by:

- Bettey, J.H. *Church & Community: the Parish Church in English Life*. (Moonraker Press, 1979).

For statistical information on the church, and an impressive sociological summary of church development over three centuries, see:

- Currie, Robert, Gilbert, Alan, and Horsley, Lee. *Churches and Church-goers: Patterns of Church Growth in the British Isles since 1700*. (Clarendon Press, 1977).

The architecture and internal fittings of Anglican churches are not dealt with in this book. There are numerous works on particular aspects of fabric such as pulpits, fonts and screens, which cannot be listed here. In addition to the work by Friar noted above, useful introductions are provided by:

- Stancliffe, David. *The Lion Companion to Church Architecture*. (Lion Hudson, 2008).
- Goodall, John. *Parish Church Treasures: the Nation's Greatest Art Collection*. (Bloomsbury, 2015).

• Taylor, Richard. *How to Read a Church: an illustrated guide to Images, Symbols and Meanings in Churches and Cathedrals.* (Rider, 2004).

Many resources for the study of Anglican history are provided by:

• Project Canterbury
  http://anglicanhistory.org

For a general introduction to sources for parish history, see:

• Bettey, J.H. *Church and Parish: a guide for local historians.* (Batsford, 1987).

An introduction to sources focused on London is provided by:

• Building on History: the Church in London
  www.open.ac.uk/Arts/building-on-history-project/ index.html

Chapter 2

THE STRUCTURE OF THE CHURCH OF ENGLAND

The Church of England claimed to be inclusive, and still attempts to live up to that claim. One of the major differences between the Church of England and other denominations is the assumption that, in the former, all parishioners are regarded as church members. Even today, all baptised parishioners are entitled to be included in the parish electoral roll if they so wish. Where Baptists require adult baptism, and Quakers require convincement, the Church of England simply requires residence.

Its inclusiveness meant that, in the past, the Church frequently acted on behalf of the State. For example, it registered baptisms, marriages and burials. When it did so, it assumed that all subjects of the Crown were members of the Church of England. Parishioners were automatically also members of their parish church; indeed, in the sixteenth and seventeenth centuries they were required by law to attend it and could suffer penalties from either Quarter Sessions or the church courts if they did not. These courts also had concurrent jurisdiction over moral offences, such as bastardy and blasphemy, although Quarter Sessions[1] could impose harsher penalties. Church and State were not regarded as separate entities.

Before the Civil War, there were few separatists. Almost everyone believed in the value of having a single unified church to which all belonged. Yes, quite a number of Puritans regarded the church as 'being but half-reformed', but most hoped for further reformation within the Church of England, rather than outside it. Only the

Roman Catholics, and a handful of sectaries, stood outside of the Church of England.

That has enormous implications for the records, for researchers using them, and for this book. On one level, everyone mentioned in Church of England records is to be regarded as an Anglican. On another level, those records do in fact record many Nonconformists and Roman Catholics. That is particularly true of those which record the penalties inflicted on them for their non-attendance at church. It is also true that many non-Anglicans served as churchwardens and in other parish offices, and probably sought to mitigate penalties inflicted on their co-religionists by using their official position. An ancestor who was a churchwarden was not necessarily an Anglican. All householders were expected to serve if called upon to do so, regardless of their personal religious views.

The structures of the Church of England have been deeply influenced by their past, and 'compounded of constant compromise mixed with seemingly perpetual precedent'. Henry VIII broke with Rome and established five new dioceses, Cranmer established its mode of worship, Elizabeth I's long reign established its initial popularity and James I established its canons and gave it the Authorised Version of the Bible. There was a foiled attempt at root and branch reform in the mid-seventeenth century, but little actually changed in the Church's ways of working between Elizabeth's reign and the nineteenth century. Some of the problems that arose have already been discussed: gentry patronage, ineffective clerical discipline, clerical dependence on tithes, unrealistic diocesan geography.

The Church of England is ruled by bishops and archbishops. Theoretically, clergy met regularly in the Convocations of Canterbury and York. Convocation had responsibility for revision of the canons. In practice there were few meetings in the late seventeenth and early eighteenth centuries, and none at all between 1741 and 1852. Reform began in the late nineteenth century, when the Lower House created a House of Laity in 1885. In 1919, Parliament granted the newly-constituted Church Assembly legislative powers over church matters, subject to Parliamentary scrutiny. The Assembly was reconstituted as the General Synod of the Church of England in 1970. There are three separate houses in the Synod: the bishops, the clergy, and the laity. Convocation continues to exist. It is formed by General Synod's Houses of Bishops and Clergy, and has the right to meet separately if it wishes.

The Archbishops of Canterbury and York have overall responsibility for both their respective provinces, and their own dioceses. Each province is divided into a number of dioceses, with their own bishops. When a see becomes vacant, its administration becomes the responsibility of the Archbishop *sede vacante* (during the vacancy).

The Archbishops were and are at the pinnacle of Church administration. They continue to operate their own courts, although these are now vestigial in comparison to what they once were. The Prerogative Courts of Canterbury and York were the most prestigious probate courts in the land, and executors frequently had wills proved there for precisely that reason. The Court of Arches hears appeals from diocesan courts. Marriage licences were once issued by the Archbishops' Vicar General, and may still be issued by his Faculty Office.

Bishops exercise jurisdiction over dioceses consisting of several hundred parishes. Working with the archdeacons and other diocesan officials, they ordain, institute and induct the clergy, supervise both them and the churchwardens, conduct visitations, and represent the church in the political life of the nation. They once proved wills, repressed Roman Catholicism and Nonconformity, and enforced standards of morality. Through the ecclesiastical courts, they exercised jurisdiction over sin, sex and probate, as one author has put it.[2] They could impose sentences of penance or excommunication; heavier sentences could only be imposed in secular courts.

Diocesan bishops may be assisted in their work by suffragan bishops, and by archdeacons. A few suffragan bishops were appointed by Elizabeth I, but thereafter they lapsed until 1870. They undertook tasks that can only be performed by bishops, such as ordination and confirmation. Archdeacons are appointed to undertake administrative tasks within their archdeaconries. They have/had responsibility for matters such as church property, the welfare of clergy, and (until 1838) the proving of wills. They conduct regular visitations of their parishes, and formerly held courts, which had their own staff. They acted as the *oculi episcopi*: the eyes of the bishop. John Head, the Archdeacon of Canterbury 1748–69, was especially active in conveying information about his archdeaconry to Archbishop Secker.[3] In the early nineteenth century, the office of rural dean, which almost disappeared after the Reformation, was re-introduced in order to support the work of the archdeacon, and to bring the clergy closer together.[4]

Cathedrals provide the bishops with their seats, but their deans and chapters operate as separate corporations, which formerly mimicked the diocesan courts in their own jurisdictions. The dean presides over a chapter consisting of various canons and prebendaries. In pre-reformation foundations, many prebendaries were non-resident, holding sinecures. Most chapters have officers such as treasurers, chancellors and precentors, drawn from the residentiary canons. There were also many minor functionaries, such as minor canons, vicars-choral, sacrists and lecturers. Many peculiars (areas outside of the normal jurisdiction of the diocesan bishop) were administered by the deans and chapters of cathedrals. Bishops, archbishops and cathedrals all possessed considerable endowments of land. Many muniments amongst their archives are in fact estate records. Their endowments were transferred to the Ecclesiastical Commission (now the Church Commissioners) in the mid-nineteenth century.

The parish is the basic unit of the Church of England.[5] Its records (especially its registers) are the first port of call for genealogical and demographic inquiries before civil registration. Every parish had its own church. The division of England into parishes mostly took place between the eighth and the thirteenth centuries, and proceeded more rapidly in the southern counties than in the north. Partly for

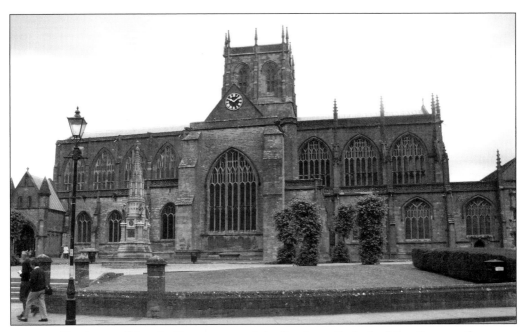

Sherborne Abbey in Dorset was originally the cathedral of the diocese of Sherborne, then a Benedictine monastery, and is now the parish church.

that reason, northern parishes tend to be larger than those in Southern England, and were frequently sub-divided into chapelries. Chapelries had their own chapels, and sometimes kept their own records. In the course of time, some became parishes in their own right.

Each parish was supposed to have its own parish priest, although in practice there were many pluralists holding several benefices. The problem of non-residence in the early nineteenth century is discussed below. Nowadays a number of parishes are frequently joined together under a 'priest in charge'. The role of the parish priest was three-fold. Firstly, he presided at Sunday worship week by week, and had responsibility for the parish's baptisms, marriages and funerals. Secondly, he had an important social role, dispensing charity, running schools, writing wills, and providing basic medical services. Thirdly, he was deeply involved in parish government, presiding at vestry meetings, reading royal proclamations, keeping an eye on the activities of overseers, certifying the orthodoxy of communicants and perhaps even serving as a Justice of the Peace.

St David's Cathedral, the centre of the church in South Wales.

When parishes were first established a thousand years ago, the priest appointed to serve them became their rector. He received the tithes – the tenth of produce – which the faithful were required to pay to the church. The living was also usually endowed with glebelands, which provided the rector with another source of income, and a rectory, in which he lived. Once appointed, the benefice was the rector's private property for life; his property rights were sometimes referred to as the 'parson's freehold'. They gave him the security 'to be prophet or saint, lover of incense or hammer of bishops'.[6]

Norman monasticism overturned much of this pattern. From the eleventh century onwards, monasteries were increasingly endowed with, and appropriated, churches. The appropriator became the institutional rector, taking the entire income of the benefice, but appointing a vicar to undertake the care of souls, perhaps paying a salary or allocating a portion of the tithes. Numerous churches were appropriated to monasteries and other religious institutions (such as cathedrals) in this way.

The dissolution of the monasteries in the sixteenth century led to the Crown seizing control of their rectories. Although it kept some in its own hands, many were purchased (the technical term is impropriated) by laymen. Lay rectors thus became entitled to tithes, and gained the advowsons, that is, the right to present to livings. By 1603, no less than 43 per cent of livings had been impropriated by lay rectors.[7] By 1836, this figure had been reduced to 20 per cent.[8] Throughout the eighteenth century, almost a half of advowsons were in lay hands, although clergy – not just the bishops, but also many parochial incumbents – had 36 per cent.[9] By 1830, 57 per cent of advowsons were in the hand of the Crown and lay patrons.[10] In the late seventeenth century, over a quarter of the clergy in the Diocese of Canterbury were the sons of gentlemen.[11] It was not, however, the county gentry who sent increasing numbers of their sons into the church in the eighteenth century. Rather, clergy of 'gentle' origins tended to come from the increasingly wealthy professional classes – merchants, doctors, lawyers – whose wealth entitled them to be regarded as gentlemen.[12]

Lay ownership of advowsons also enabled a different approach to patronage. In the early seventeenth century, the Feoffees for Impropriations (a group of Puritan laymen) began to purchase advowsons so that they could present Puritanically-minded clergy to them. Archbishop Laud put a stop to their activities, but the idea was resurrected by Charles Simeon in the early nineteenth century. The Simeon Trustees still appoint evangelicals in 160 livings.

Many priests also purchased former monastic advowsons in order to obtain a living. Clergy who owned advowsons were not allowed to present themselves. However, they frequently granted the right of presentation to a friend so that he could present the grantee.[13] It has been calculated that in 1878 perhaps one advowson in eighteen was held by the incumbent.[14]

Clergy ownership of advowsons also enabled married priests to make provision for their sons. The family advowson sometimes led to the creation of clerical dynasties, allowing successive members of the same family to succeed each other in the same living for several generations. Clerical dynasties were also created when clergy sent their offspring to the University with the hope that they would be able to find a living for themselves. Many clerics bequeathed their libraries to their sons, indicating their hope that they would follow their father's calling. Some 31 per cent of Leicestershire parish incumbents of 1670 were able to send their eldest sons into the clergy.[15]

The income of the clergy came predominantly from tithes (see Chapter 6), and from the glebe. For some clergy, income from teaching was also important. Clergy sometimes benefited from surplice fees (for conducting baptisms, marriages and burials). Some also received Easter offerings, and topped their incomes up in other ways. The value of tithes rose dramatically in the eighteenth century. Dependence on tithes meant dependence on the prosperity of agriculture. Agricultural innovation increased profits for farmers – and tithes for clergy. Steam-driven pumps in the Fens helped to increase the value of the vicarage of Wisbech from £180 in 1716 to £2,000 in the early nineteenth century.[16] The Napoleonic Wars boosted tithes by increasing agricultural prices. The enclosure of open fields frequently meant the commutation of tithes in return for a grant of land, giving incumbents much higher incomes.

The assessment and collection of tithes was sometimes very problematic. The duty of the clergy to provide spiritual care for their parishioners could easily be stymied by demands for tithes. Tithe disputes could poison parish life. Clergymen demanding what they considered to be their rightful dues occasionally gained a reputation which damaged their ability to perform their pastoral duties. Many clergy tried to mollify their farmers by holding annual tithe dinners. But it was difficult to escape the apparent incompatibility between the roles of spiritual counsellor and tax collector.

The enclosure movement provided a way for incumbents to

escape this dilemma. Tithes were just as problematic for tithe-paying farmers as they were for the clergy. Farmers wanting to enclose open fields needed the consent of everyone holding property rights in those fields, usually including the clergy. Their consent could be won, and tithes extinguished, by granting them generous allotments of land. Frequently, the incumbent's legal, fencing, and drainage costs of enclosure were met by the other proprietors. Enclosure, accompanied by the commutation of tithe, took place in about 2,200 parishes. Between 1757 and 1835, over 185,000 acres were added to glebe lands. Some clergy doubled their incomes.

It has been estimated that between 1770 and 1840, the incomes of benefices increased by 400 per cent.[17] In the same period, inflation was c.100 per cent. Pluralism was also much rifer in 1840 than it had been in 1700. At the beginning of the eighteenth century, perhaps one clergyman in six held more than one living; by 1840 the figure was perhaps one in three. Too few priests had been ordained in the mid- to late eighteenth century to fill all the positions available. The incomes of individual clergymen must have increased by an astonishing 700 per cent in the period. The median annual income of a clergyman in 1830 was £275. There were, however, wide divergences. A third of clergy made do with incomes between £60 and £180; another third had over £400. Some benefices were so poor that their incumbents had to be pluralists in order to obtain an income that would enable them to live as a clergyman should. But even the poorest clergy were amongst the richest 15 per cent of the population.

Many clergymen were able to live in the style of gentlemen. The evidence of the prosperity of the top third can still be seen: the house name 'Old Rectory' is frequently still attached to the grandiose piles built by newly-enriched clergymen in the late eighteenth and early nineteenth centuries. Most were too expensive to maintain, and were sold off by a much poorer church in the late twentieth century.[18]

Conversely, of course, the accommodation of the poorer clergy left much to be desired. In 1833, no less than 2,878 benefices lacked any accommodation at all; another 1,728 parsonages were labelled

The eighteenth-century rectory at Epworth in Lincolnshire, built by John Wesley's father.

'unfit'.[19] Expectations, of course, had increased; what was 'unfit' in 1833 would frequently have been regarded as perfectly acceptable a century earlier. Nevertheless, many clergy who did not have a 'fit' parsonage did not reside on their cures. The same applied to many wealthier incumbents who did have a decent parsonage. Non-residence was a major problem; only four benefices in ten had a resident incumbent in 1813.[20] A few non-residents lived close enough to be 'virtually resident', and performed their duties themselves. Most employed a curate, or paid a neighbouring incumbent to undertake their 'duty'. Many curates were effectively in charge of their parishes.

The word 'curate' also had other meanings. A curate could be a preacher employed by a borough, or a charity, outside of formal ecclesiastical structures. 'Perpetual curates' were effectively incumbents, possessing permanent tenure of chapelries. It was not until the nineteenth century that the designation 'curate' came to be applied primarily to trainee priests.

Increasing clerical incomes, and non-residence, meant that the social distance between priests and their congregations gradually increased. This was symbolized by the fact that, increasingly, parsonages boasted studies and books. Most medieval parochial clergy had little more education than their parishioners. The Reformation, however, required educated preachers to spread the Gospel. By the time of the Civil War most clergymen had attended university. In the eighteenth century, the clergy were increasingly gentrified.

The lower classes did not disappear from the ranks of the clergy completely; in the late eighteenth century 27.5 per cent of clergy in the Diocese of Canterbury were 'plebians', the sons of tradesmen or professionals.[21] By the 1830s, perhaps one-fifth of the clergy were related to gentle and aristocratic families. Another fifth were from clerical dynasties. Perhaps 15 per cent came from professional backgrounds. The remainder came from a wide range of different backgrounds, a few of them very humble.[22] In the decade after 1834, perhaps 90 per cent of ordinands were graduates.[23] Many 'plebians' bought their sons a university education, encouraging them to take orders that placed them on a par with the gentry. The poor were right to believe that many clergy made 'rather a good thing out of their jobs'.[24]

The wealth and education of the clergy meant that they had to be taken seriously as a part of the governing classes. In 1689, Edward Chamberlayne argued that 'who so proper to make and keep peace as they whose constant duty it is to preach peace'.[25] In 1761, no fewer than 1,038 clergymen were serving as Justices of the Peace.[26] By 1834, a fourth of the magistrates in England were clergymen; one clergyman in six was a Justice of the Peace, although it is important to appreciate that many clerical Justices were members of long-established gentry families.[27]

Late eighteenth- and early nineteenth-century clergy were credited with doing almost the whole of the work of the magistracy.[28] Their responsibility for the maintenance of order did not sit easily with their pastoral role, despite Chamberlayne's comment. The clerical magistrates involved in summoning the Yeomanry at the Peterloo Massacre of 1819 attracted intense opprobrium. Demands for tithes, increasing poverty and post-war depression led to the clergy becoming increasingly unpopular. Many were threatened during the unrest of 1830–1.[29] The pastoral mission of the church could not be performed in the face of such unpopularity.

However, this unpopularity was not to continue. Nor were the other abuses of the eighteenth century. The Stipendiary Curates Act of 1813 required non-resident clergy to appoint curates in their absence.[30] From the 1830s, the number of clerical Justices of the Peace steadily declined. It began to be recognized that the roles of pastor and judge were incompatible. The Pluralities Acts of 1838 and 1850 put a gradual end to excessive pluralism and non-residence, reducing clergy incomes in the process, although those who were already pluralists were not affected.

These Acts dramatically changed the position of curates. They ceased to have sole charge of parishes, and became merely assistants to incumbents. In consequence, the Stipendiary Curates Act of 1813 ceased to protect their incomes (since they were not 'in charge' as required by that Act). The 1838 Act did, however, give them greater security of tenure, since it required their dismissal to be sanctioned by their bishop. Most nineteenth- and twentieth-century curates were trainees.

The ancient antagonism between farmers and clergy over tithe was lifted by the Tithe Commutation Act of 1836. Tithe in kind was converted into monetary payments, in accordance with a formula which could not be easily disputed. For almost half a century, clergy profited from continuing agricultural prosperity. However, the reform left them exposed to variations in the price of agricultural produce. When prices plummeted in the 1880s, so did the incomes of the clergy. They lost perhaps a third of their income. Those who relied on their glebe were, perhaps, the worst hit, as they could not find tenants. Many did not possess the skills needed to farm themselves.[31] It was the church's worst financial crisis since the sixteenth century. An 1893 report stated that 'this clerical distress is not only very severe, but also widespread, and . . . has been borne with the noble spirit of patient endurance'.[32] In response, the custom began of presenting the clergy with a collection made on Easter Day. The clergy may have become poorer, but they had also become more popular.

The number of ordinations increased dramatically in the nineteenth century. Where there had been an average of 245 per annum in the mid-eighteenth century, in the 1820s there were 530.[33] At the same time, however, the proportion of graduate clergy was decreasing. By 1900, 35 per cent of ordinands were non-graduates.[34] Many clergy were being trained in the Church's own theological colleges, and the clergy were becoming professionalized. The decline in the number of graduates may also reflect the declining income of the clergy.

The demands imposed on the laity, however, steadily increased. The administration of parish ecclesiastical responsibilities was placed in the hands of two churchwardens in each parish. According to the 1604 canons, one was to be chosen by the vestry, one by the incumbent. In practice, custom frequently decided who should be appointed. Sometimes, the choice was made according to a rota of heads of households. In other places, the decision might be left to the retiring churchwardens.

Churchwardens' roles expanded over the centuries. Ecclesiastical duties included keeping order during services, collecting church rates, and attending visitations of bishops and archdeacons. They were responsible for making sure that everything required for the conduct of services was available, for example, service books, communion plate, bread, wine, vestments and musical instruments. They paid parish servants such as the organist, the verger, and the parish clerk. They regularly presented sexual offenders, those who failed to attend church, and executors who failed to obtain probate, at the visitations of archdeacons and bishops (see below, pp.109–11).

They also acquired secular duties. Tudor and Stuart legislation assigned numerous tasks to them, ranging from poor relief to the detection of recusancy, from vermin eradication to highway maintenance. Under the Elizabethan Poor Law Acts of 1597 and 1602, they became *ex officio* overseers of the poor. They worked closely with other overseers, with parish constables, and with highway surveyors. They also worked closely with parish vestries, which played a major role in the appointment of all parish officers. It was not until the nineteenth century that sacred and secular functions began to be separated. Vestries continued to operate until 1919, by which time their secular powers had been lost to other local authorities. They were replaced by Parochial Church Councils, which are now responsible for church fabric, for the organization of parochial activities, and for financial matters. Churchwardens' accounts and vestry minutes record much information about their activities, and will be discussed in Chapter 6. These records are, of course, supplemented by Diocesan archives, discussed in Chapter 7.

The work of the other parish officers was primarily of a secular nature; their records are discussed elsewhere.[35] Churchwardens were drawn from the laity, as were the other parish officers whose work was of a more secular nature. The parish provided a range of benefits to the laity, including the provision of a church and a priest. In return, a range of sometimes onerous duties were imposed upon them, such as the duty to serve in parish office when required, to pay rates, and to attend church. Attendance at Sunday services was compulsory until 1688. The canons expected parishioners to receive communion at least three times each year, although many were more infrequent communicants. The ritual was regarded with awe; it was popularly thought that it was only for the holy. Those who thought themselves insufficiently holy did not attend.[36]

Whilst in church, the laity were expected to be reverent. The *Book of Common Prayer* required them to pay attention to the services, to say the responses, and perhaps to sing psalms or hymns. The parish clerk,[37] or perhaps a choir, might lead the responses and the singing, but they merely responded to the clergyman leading the service. Otherwise, the role of the laity was passive. That was to change. In the nineteenth century, increasing demands on the clergy meant that they needed the assistance of laymen in their ministry. By 1850, most London churches had their own lay visiting societies. The creation of lay readers in the 1860s, and the experience of Wilson Carlisle in using laymen for the work of the Church Army in the 1880s, caused a gradual relaxation of centuries-old Anglican opposition towards lay ministry. Women were also catered for; in 1862, the Bishop of London ordained deaconesses to support his parochial clergy. By 1900, there were also sixty communities of Anglican nuns.[38]

There have since been many changes to the position of the clergy. The ordination of women priests, and the disposal of grandiose eighteenth-century rectories, are perhaps the most visible. The effective abolition of the parson's freehold may prove to be just as significant in the future. Much church property is now vested in the Church Commissioners, who pay clergy pensions. Glebe properties were vested in Diocesan Boards of Finance in 1976. Clergy stipends have become the responsibility of dioceses, raised by a levy on parishes known as the 'share'. Dioceses also provide clergy housing. Pluralism has ceased to be seen as a problem; rather, it has become the solution to the lack of finance and low clergy numbers. Under the Pastoral Measure of 1968, parishes have been joined together in 'team ministries' under 'priests in charge', who run their benefices with the aid of non-stipendiary clergy and lay readers. The benefice, rather than the parish, is increasingly the focus of local church life and administration.

There are numerous exceptions to the pattern of ecclesiastical government outlined above. In particular, peculiars were numerous. It has already been noted that these were places not under the normal jurisdiction of the diocesan bishop or the local archdeacon. Some were extra-parochial, that is, they had never been assigned to a parish. These were sometimes remote areas of waste land, such as No Mans Heath (Warwickshire) and Lundy (Devon). Others included Oxbridge colleges, the Inns of Court and similar establishments, whose hierarchies exercised jurisdiction.

Parishes could also be peculiars. Bierton (Buckinghamshire), for example, was under the jurisdiction of the Dean and Chapter of Lincoln Cathedral. Peculiar jurisdiction could also be exercised by secular lords. The Crown had (and still has) direct jurisdiction over Westminster Abbey, St George's Chapel, Windsor, and a number of other institutions. At Cockington (Devon), the manorial lord had jurisdiction over probate. Most peculiars were abolished during the mid-nineteenth century.

It is important to be aware of peculiars. They did not have to send transcripts of parish registers to their diocesan bishops, many had jurisdiction over probate, and many issued marriage licences. The resultant records are usually held amongst their own archives, and not amongst diocesan records.

Dioceses, archdeaconries, parishes and peculiar jurisdictions are fully mapped in:

• Humphery-Smith, Cecil. *The Phillimore Atlas and Index of Parish Registers*. (3rd ed. Phillimore, 2003).

Numerous Anglican charities and missionary societies operated outside of the church hierarchy. So did the religious orders, which were re-introduced into the Church of England in the late nineteenth century, after a lapse of some 300 years. They were not fully accepted by the hierarchy until the First World War. The archives of these various institutions are discussed in Chapter 9.

Legally, the Church operated (and still operates) according to canon law. Canons approved in 1604 remained in force until 1964, apart from a few minor nineteenth-century tweaks. The canons were binding on the clergy, but could not override common and statute law. They are printed in:

- Bray, Gerald, ed. *The Anglican Canons, 1529-1947*. (Church of England Record Society, 6. 1998).

For an eighteenth-century handbook of canon law, the ninth edition of which was published in 1842, see:

- Burn, Richard. *Ecclesiastical Law*. (1763). (various editions available online)

Chapter 3

PRELIMINARIES TO RESEARCH: USING RECORD OFFICES, BOOKS, LIBRARIES AND THE INTERNET

This book is concerned primarily with using Church of England sources to trace ancestors who were at least nominally Anglicans, and to trace the histories of local churches. If you are researching ancestors, it is assumed that you have already discovered as much information from your elderly relatives as you can. Some familiarity with other more general sources of genealogical information, such as the records of civil registration and the census, is also assumed. If you are new to family history, then you should read one of the many excellent general introductions currently available. There are far too many to list here, but the most comprehensive is:

• Herber, Mark. *Ancestral Trails: the Complete Guide to British Genealogy and Family History.* (2nd ed. Sutton Publishing/ Society of Genealogists, 2004).

For a useful dictionary encyclopaedia, see:

• Few, Janet. *The Family Historian's Enquire Within.* (6th ed. Family History Partnership, 2014).

Record offices, libraries and the internet are the prime workshops of family and local historians. It is important to know which institutions/websites are likely to be most useful, what information they can provide and how they should be used. Original documents produced by parishes and dioceses will normally be held in local record offices, and printed books in libraries, although the modern trend is to amalgamate the two into one institution. That course has been followed in recent years in Devon, Somerset and Wiltshire, just to name the counties with which I am most familiar.

RECORD OFFICES

Record offices are warehouses for archives. Indeed, they are sometimes referred to as archives, but the word is probably better kept to refer to the actual documents. Archives provide almost all the written evidence we need to trace our ancestors. Most, of course, were not written for that purpose, although parish registers (see Chapter 4) and civil registers are important exceptions to that rule. Without archives, most genealogical books could not have been written, and the internet would be of little use to genealogists.

There are numerous record offices, both local and national. County record offices were originally created to house the records of Quarter Sessions, but are now likely to hold both parish and diocesan records – although where dioceses covered more than one county, the diocesan archives will not normally be split between the relevant record offices. For example, although the Diocese of Exeter included both Devon and Cornwall, its archives are held by Devon Heritage Trust, not Cornwall Record Office, although the latter does hold Archdeaconry of Cornwall records. Many smaller areas also have their own record offices, for example, Barnstaple's North Devon Record Office. Where these exist, parish records may have been deposited in them. All local record offices also hold a wide range of private family and estate papers, which may include, for example, the correspondence of clergy.

There are also a range of national record offices. Of these, the most significant for our purposes is:

The National Archives.

• The National Archives
  www.nationalarchives. gov.uk

It holds a variety of records relating to the clergy, and also to the loyalty of churchmen, as well as more general holdings such as the State Papers Domestic, which record many activities of churchmen.

   Another important institution, whose manuscripts catalogue is always worth searching, is:

• The British Library
  www.bl.uk

Other national record offices relevant to our purpose include:

• Lambeth Palace Library
  www.lambethpalacelibrary.org
  Depository for Province of Canterbury archives.

- The Church of England Record Centre
  www.lambethpalacelibrary.org/content/cerc
  Holds the records of the central bodies of the Church of England,
  including those of the Church Commissioners and the National
  Society. Administered by Lambeth Palace Library.
- Pusey House
  www.puseyhouse.org.uk
  Holds the archives of a number of Anglo-Catholic societies and
  religious orders, as well as the papers of many Anglican
  churchmen of the nineteenth and twentieth centuries. There are
  c.2,300 photographs of nineteenth-century clergymen. Reports
  and papers from General Synod are also held.
- Church of England: CCB Library [Cathedral and Church
  Buildings]
  **www.churchofengland.org/about-us/our-buildings/helping-
  you/library.aspx**
  Focuses on ecclesiastical architecture, art, design and liturgy;
  holds survey files on over 16,000 parish churches.
- Borthwick Institute for Archives
  www.york.ac.uk/borthwick
  Holds archives of the Northern Province (the Archdiocese of
  York).

Other record offices are mentioned below. For a detailed listing of
over 400 record offices, visit:

- Find an archive in the UK and beyond
  http://discovery.nationalarchives.gov.uk/find-an-archive

Union catalogues list records held in numerous institutions. Begin
by searching:

- The National Archives Discovery catalogue
  http://discovery.nationalarchives.gov.uk

For archives held by colleges and universities, see:

- Archives Hub
  www.archiveshub.ac.uk

Archives in London repositories are listed in:

- AIM 25
  www.aim25.ac.uk

For Wales, see:

- Archives Wales
  www.archivesnetworkwales.info

More detailed discussions are provided by:

- Emmison, F.G. *Introduction to Archives*. (Phillimore & Co., 1978).
- Iredale, David. *Enjoying Archives: What they Are; Where to Find Them; How to Use Them*. (Phillimore, 1985).
- Lumas, Sue. *Basic Facts about . . . Archives*. (Federation of Family History Societies, 1997).

BOOKS AND LIBRARIES

Books are important to family historians. You need to know how to find them, and what they might tell you. In general, books will give you far more detailed and authoritative guidance than websites. I have already suggested that you should read an introductory guide if you are researching family history. There are also innumerable transcripts, calendars and indexes of original documents in printed form, many of which are not available on the internet. Brief biographies of millions – yes, millions – of individuals are contained in biographical dictionaries. Publishers such as Pen & Sword, the Society of Genealogists, the Family History Partnership and the Federation of Family History Societies (to name but a few) have

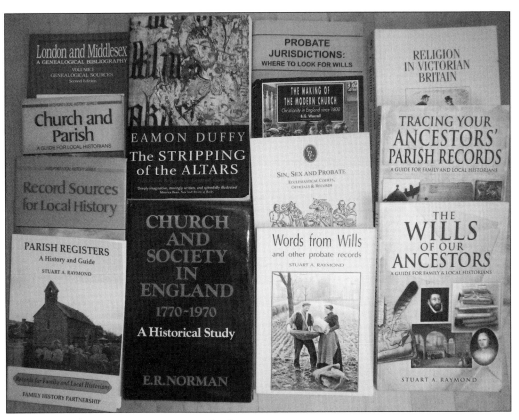

Books – invaluable sources of information.

issued numerous guides to particular categories of source material. County record societies have issued numerous transcripts, calendars, and indexes of original sources. So have local family history societies. The websites of these publishers provide much useful information on books currently available.

In order to find relevant books, consult library catalogues and bibliographies. The standard bibliography for family historians, now somewhat out of date, but still useful, is:

• Raymond, Stuart A. *English Genealogy: a Bibliography*. (3rd ed. Federation of Family History Societies, 1996).

This volume is accompanied by a series of county bibliographies by the same author, which cover Buckinghamshire, Cheshire, Cornwall,

Cumberland and Westmorland, Devon, Dorset, Essex, Hampshire, Lancashire, Lincolnshire, London and Middlesex, Norfolk, Oxfordshire, Somerset, Suffolk, Surrey and Sussex, Wiltshire, and Yorkshire.

For county record society publications, see:

• Royal Historical Society: National and Regional History
http://royalhistsoc.org/publications/national-regional-history

Some 16,000 biographical dictionaries are listed in:

• Slocum, R.B. *Biographical dictionaries and related works: an international bibliography of more than 16,000 collective biographies, bio-bibliographies, collections of epitaphs, selected genealogical works, dictionaries of acronyms and pseudonyms, material in government manuals, bibliographies of biography, biographical indexes, and selected portrait catalogs.* (2 vols. 2nd ed. Detroit: Gale Research, 1986).

Millions of entries are included in:

• *Biography and genealogy master index: a consolidated index to more than 3,200,000 biographical sketches in over 350 current and retrospective biographical dictionaries.* (Gale Biographical Index Series 1. 8 vols. 2nd ed. Detroit: Gale, 1980. Supplements 1981–5, 1986–90, and annually from 1991).

Numerous biographies of clergy and other churchmen are included in the

• Oxford Dictionary of National Biography
www.oxforddnb.com
(A printed edition is also available)

Once you have identified needed books, you can either purchase them, or search catalogues to locate them in libraries. You might find them in a wide variety of different libraries. Most counties and large towns have a local studies library, collecting publications relating to its own area, and sometimes also holding more general works such as the present volume. University and college libraries, especially those with history departments, sometimes have collections useful to family and local historians. Many family history societies have useful libraries. Most counties have an archaeological and/or historical society with a library; many hold relevant material.

The catalogues of most public and university libraries are online, and can be consulted on the following union catalogues:

The library of St Paul's Cathedral in 1893.

- OCLC World Cat
  www.worldcat.org
- Copac
  http://copac.jisc.ac.uk

Family history society library catalogues are sometimes available online. For a list of these societies and their websites, visit:

- Federation of Family History Societies: Member Societies
  www.ffhs.org.uk/members2/england/eng-beds.php

The Society of Genealogists deserves a separate mention, as it has the largest library in the country devoted solely to genealogy (although the British Library's genealogical collection may be larger). Its website also has a large collection of digitized transcripts and indexes of original source, although they are only available to members. Visit:

- Society of Genealogists
  www.sog.org.uk

The Family History Centres of the Latter Day Saints, which can be found throughout the world as well as in the UK, have access to the huge microfilm collections housed in the Church's Family History Library. Its website also has a substantial number of digitized images of original sources, which are free to access, but rival in size some of the commercial hosts listed below. Visit:

- Family Search
  https://familysearch.org

Some local archaeological and historical societies have online catalogues, although bear in mind that these are not necessarily complete. Others do not have online catalogues, but may still be worth contacting. An online directory of societies is provided by:

- Local History Online: Directory of Local History and Allied Societies
  www.local-history.co.uk/Groups

For more detailed guides to using libraries, see:

- Raymond, Stuart A. *Using Libraries: Workshops for Family Historians.* (Federation of Family Historians, 2001).
- Winterbotham, Diana, and Crosby, Alan. *The Local Studies Library: a Handbook for Local Historians.* (British Association for Local History, 1998).

Many books (including some mentioned below) can be read on the internet. A number of websites are dedicated to providing access to digitized copies of out of print books. These include:

- Internet Archive
  https://archive.org
- Hathi Trust Digital Library
  http://babel.hathitrust.org/cgi/mb
- Open Library
  https://openlibrary.org
- Google Books
  https://books.google.co.uk

THE INTERNET
In the last two decades, the internet has transformed genealogical research, to such an extent that many genealogists do not think of looking anywhere else. That is a bad mistake. Despite the advent of huge collections of digitized images, record offices and libraries continue to hold far more archives and books than are available on the web. Nevertheless, a huge amount of information is available online. General introductions to the internet for genealogists include:

- Christian, Peter. *The Genealogist's Internet: the Essential Guide to Researching Your Family History Online.* (5th ed. Bloomsbury, 2012).
- Paton, Chris. *Tracing Your Family History on the Internet: a Guide for Family Historians.* (2nd ed. Pen & Sword, 2014).

The best websites for family historians are listed in:

- Scott, Jonathan. *The Family History Web Directory.* (Pen & Sword, 2015).

Reference may also be made to:

- Cyndi's List of Genealogy Sites on the Web
  http://cyndislist.com

The major genealogical site for the UK is

- Genuki
  www.genuki.org.uk

This site includes separate pages for each county and parish in England and Wales. Within those pages, subject headings such as 'church records' and 'church history' provide much information of relevance to Anglican research, sometimes including transcripts and indexes of relevant records.

A number of commercial sites host huge collections of digitized images of original sources, including many parish registers. The most important of these are:

- Ancestry
  www.ancestry.co.uk
- Find My Past
  www.findmypast.co.uk
- The Genealogist
  www.thegenealogist.co.uk

It is worth noting that some public and academic libraries offer free access to selected commercial websites. Other relevant websites are listed at appropriate points throughout this book.

HANDWRITING AND LATIN

Archives are generally written documents, although printed forms, such as those used for compiling marriage registers after 1754, were sometimes used. Handwriting varies considerably and has also changed over the centuries. At first sight, seventeenth-century handwriting may appear to be unreadable to the twenty-first century reader; sixteenth-century handwriting is even more difficult, and the fact that some pre-eighteenth century records are in Latin may put you off completely. But always remember that documents were written in order to be read! Seventeenth-century handwriting is really not that difficult if you are prepared to put in some practice. If you can manage to read one or two words, you can identify the letter forms used, and look for them in the remainder of the document.

In the medieval period, documents were usually written in Latin. This practice was gradually phased out during the sixteenth and seventeenth centuries, but still occasionally survived in the early eighteenth century. This should not be too much of a problem. Latin may be encountered in early parish registers. Entries, however, generally follow a common form, and use the same words repeatedly. It is easy to identify the Latin words for 'was baptised' (baptizata fuit), 'was married' (nupta fuit), and 'was buried' (sepulta fuit).

There are a number of useful guides to help you understand both old handwriting and Latin. Letter forms are illustrated in:

• Buck, W.S.B. *Examples of Handwriting, 1550-1750*. (Society of Genealogists, 2008).

The National Archives website offers a useful tutorial:

• Palaeography: reading old handwriting, 1500 – 1800: A practical online tutorial
  www.nationalarchives.gov.uk/palaeography

For a more detailed guide, see:

- Marshall, Hilary. *Palaeography for Family and Local Historians.* (2nd ed. Phillimore, 2010).

See also:

- Grieve, Hilda E.P. *Examples of English Handwriting, 1150-1750, with transcripts and translations.* (2nd ed. Essex Record Office, 1959).

For Latin, the best introductory guide is:

- Beginners' Latin: Latin 1086 – 1733: a practical online tutorial for beginners
  www.nationalarchives.gov.uk/latin/beginners

Useful handbooks are provided by:

- Morris, Janet. *A Latin Glossary for Family and Local Historians.* (Amended ed. Family History Partnership, 2009).
- Westcott, Brooke. *Making Sense of Latin Documents for Family & Local Historians.* (Family History Partnership, 2015).

For a more detailed introduction to medieval Latin, see:

- Stuart, Denis. *Latin for Local and Family Historians: a Beginners' Guide.* (Phillimore, 1995).

Innumerable abbreviations were used by Latinist scribes. For these, together with a Latin glossary, and lists of Latin forenames and place-names, see:

- Martin, Charles Trice. *The Record Interpreter.* (2nd ed. Phillimore, 1982). Originally published 1910.

ASSESSING THE EVIDENCE

Begin by establishing where your evidence came from. That should enable you to judge its reliability. Genealogists frequently find evidence in the form of transcripts, indexes, calendars, microfilm, databases, webpages, digitized images and the printed page. It is vital to appreciate that these are all entirely dependent on the original source, which is likely to be a handwritten page. You must judge whether the form in which you find your evidence is an accurate copy of the original. Be aware that transcribers and indexers make many mistakes; if you find a transcript that is 95 per cent accurate you are doing well.

You need to be aware what is meant by some of the terms just used. A transcript should be an exact copy, word by word, letter by letter, of the original document. A calendar, in this context, is a summary of an original document, giving the gist of the information it contains, but not necessarily providing all the information you need. An index is merely a list of terms, indicating where those terms can be found in the original document. It should never be regarded as providing all the evidence in the document indexed. A printed transcript is merely a copy of a handwritten or typed transcript made by a typesetter, and has less authority than the original transcript, even if a digitized image has been made of it. If you see a webpage that misuses these terms – especially 'transcript' and 'index' – then you will know that the webmaster knows less about what he is doing than you do, and will question the evidence he provides accordingly.

Increasingly, digitized images of original sources are becoming available on the internet. Digitized parish registers and probate records can frequently be found. These are likely to be more accurate than any transcript – although the camera does miss pages, and may not show what is on the back of the document photographed.

Chapter 4

PARISH REGISTERS OF BAPTISMS, MARRIAGES AND BURIALS

A. THE HISTORY OF PARISH REGISTERS

Parish registers of baptisms, marriages, and burials are one of the few genealogical sources originally created to aid genealogical research. The official reason given for keeping them was 'to avoid dispute touching ages, titles, or lineal descents'.[1] In a society where land tenure depended on inheritance, the property owners of sixteenth-century England needed to ensure that they could prove their title to the land they had inherited.

Other motives for the introduction of parish registers were rumoured, however. Contemporaries thought it likely that the Crown intended to use them to tax baptisms, marriages and burials. That rumour helped to inspire the Pilgrimage of Grace. Regardless of their instigator's intention, they were not far wrong; two centuries after their introduction they were used for precisely that purpose, as we will see.

Thomas Cromwell was well-travelled in Europe before he joined the household of Cardinal Wolsey, and, subsequently, became Henry VIII's first minister and 'vicegerent', in charge of the Church. He probably adopted the idea of keeping parish registers because he had seen them being kept whilst on the Continent. In his 1538 injunctions, he ordered all parish priests to

> kepe one boke or registere wherein ye shall write the day and yere of every weddying christenyng and buryeng made within yor parishe for your tyme, and so everyman suceedyng you

Broadhembury – a rural Devon church with its graveyard.

likewise And shall there insert every persons name that shalbe so weddid christened or buryed And for the sauff keepinge of the same boke the parishe shalbe bonde to provide of these comen charges one sure coffer with twoo lockes and keys whereof the one to remayne with you, and the other with the said wardens, wherein the saide boke shalbe laide upp. Whiche boke ye shall every Sonday take furthe and in the presence of the said wardens or one of them write and recorde in the same all the weddinges christenynges and buryenges made the hole weke befire. And that done to lay upp the boke in the said coffer as afore.[2]

This was but one of the many injunctions that Cromwell issued at this time. Most were Protestant. Many were tightened up and made more Protestant during Edward VI's reign, but most were discarded by Queen Mary. Her ministers, however, retained this one, indeed improved it. In 1555, Cardinal Pole issued an injunction requiring parish priests to record the names of godparents. He followed it up in 1557 by asking 'whether they do keep the book of registers of christenings, buryings, and marriages, with the names of the godfathers and godmothers'.[3] Marian registers frequently recorded the names of godparents, but this feature is obscured by the fact that most surviving sixteenth-century registers are copies made at the end of the century. These copies did not necessarily include everything in the original registers, and seem to have deliberately excluded godparents. One of the few surviving registers which list them is that for Banbury, edited by Jeremy Gibson.[4] When Elizabeth re-issued the injunction in 1559, the clause mentioning godparents was omitted.

Cromwell's injunctions were not always obeyed. Some registers commence in 1538, others not until 1547, suggesting that the injunctions were ignored until Edward VI re-issued them. Sadly, only a small proportion of sixteenth-century registers survive. Sadly, too, a new canon introduced in 1598, and again in 1604, which was meant to preserve them, in practice had the effect of diminishing their usefulness. Every parish was ordered to purchase a new parchment book, to replace the old paper registers. Entries in the old registers were to be transcribed into the new book 'since the time that the law was first made in that behalf', but 'especially since the beginning of the reign of the late queen', i.e. Elizabeth.[5] The wording was unfortunate; many took it to mean that they did not need to bother about transcribing pre-1558 registers. Few of the old paper registers survive, and it is likely that some details in them were not transcribed at all, as we have seen was the case with the entries relating to godparents. At St Dunstans in the West, both the old paper register, and its parchment replacement, survive. A comparison of the entries in the two volumes is illuminating. An entry in the original register dated 17 February 1560/1 reads: 'Mr Rithe buried. A bencher of Lyncolnes Yne, buryed out of the newe brycke byldynge beynge in owre p'ishe, the hether syde of Lyncolnes Yne'. Its counterpart in the parchment register is heavily abbreviated: 'Mr. Rithe buried.'[6]

One feature of these transcripts may mislead the unwary. Entries for each year were frequently signed by the parish priest and churchwardens. The signatures were not, however, of those in office for that year, but rather of those in office when the transcript was made. They provide no proof of the longevity in office of those who signed.

Apart from the godparents of Mary's reign, registers of the sixteenth and seventeenth centuries were not required to follow any particular format. Entries could include as much or as little information as the scribe wished. They could be very elaborate, as has just been seen in the case of Mr. Rithe. On the other hand, entries could be terse in the extreme. For example, the register of Week St. Mary, Cornwall, records 'Buried Thomas Beaford', with the date 4 May 1602. Entries might also be intermingled with a variety of other matter. The register of Battlefield (Shropshire) opens with a list of church officers appointed between 1665 and 1672. For Wiltshire, there are so many extraneous entries in parish registers that a whole volume of the Wiltshire Record Society's publications is devoted to them.[7]

Parish registers continued to be kept throughout the reigns of James I and Charles I. There continued to be no consistency in the information that was included. Furthermore, the canon requiring registers to be written up every Sunday was frequently ignored in practice. Details of events were often scribbled into rough notebooks or scraps of paper, and written up later, perhaps once a year prior to the archdeacon's visitation, or when the bishops' transcripts (see Chapter 5) were sent into the diocesan registry. They could even be copied from the bishops' transcripts, rather than the other way around. Such practices evidently remained common until the early nineteenth century, as they were expressly forbidden by Rose's 1812 Act.

That, however, is getting ahead of the story. After civil war broke out in 1642, many registers were neglected. War was not conducive to good record-keeping. In 1645, Parliament tried to remedy the situation by ordering that each parish should keep 'a fair register book of velim',[8] recording not just dates of baptism and burial, but also the dates of births and deaths. Baptismal entries were to record the names of parents. Few surviving registers from the years following include all these details.

Reforms introduced during the Interregnum were much more revolutionary. In 1653, marriage became a civil matter, conducted before a Justice of the Peace. Banns were to be called on three successive Sundays, either in church or in the adjoining market place. They were recorded in the registers, where births and deaths were also recorded. Registers were to be kept by a lay parish officer, confusingly called the 'parish register'.

Interregnum registers were generally well kept. However, the 'Act' of 1653 was regarded as null and void by the Restoration regime after 1660. The Interregnum registers were not regarded as having any validity, even if they were handed over to the restored clergy by the lay 'parish register'. Many were lost in consequence. A special Act had to be passed to regularize marriages conducted before Justices of the Peace.

In the years following the Restoration, parish registers frequently record many more baptisms than is normal. This does not signify a post-Restoration baby boom. Rather, it reflects the fact that many babies were not baptised during the Interregnum. The restored clergy saw to it that the un-baptised youngsters in their parishes received baptism. Many must have been five or ten years old, perhaps older, at baptism. Indeed, a new office 'for the baptism of such as are of riper years' was approved by Convocation in 1661. Neither Baptists nor Quakers accepted infant baptism, so those who conformed to the Church of England needed to be baptised as adults. Adult baptisms are not necessarily recorded as such in parish registers, and provide a trap for the unwary genealogist who tries to treat such entries as surrogates for birth entries.

After 1660, there was little change in the way parish registers were kept for almost a century. In 1666, and again in 1678,

Babies have been baptised in this font at Avebury in Wiltshire for almost a millennium.

Another ancient font at Fontmell Magna in Dorset.

The church at Poundstock in Cornwall. Parts of the church date from the thirteenth century.

Parliament acted to support the cloth industry by ordering that burials should take place in a woollen shroud. Affidavits certifying compliance with the law were required. They were sometimes recorded in parish registers. In some parishes, these Acts triggered the purchase of a new volume to record entries. Alternatively, separate books of affidavits might be kept, or printed forms used. These occasionally survive amongst parish records.

In 1694, the fears voiced by Tudor rebels were realized: a tax was imposed on births, marriages and deaths, and collection was based on parish register entries. Incumbents were instructed to expand the coverage of registers by including all births, not just those which were followed by Church of England baptisms. The instruction was rarely obeyed, the authorities found it difficult to collect the tax, and the number of babies being brought for baptism declined. After repeal in 1705, an Act of Indemnity was passed to indemnify the numerous clergy who had failed to collect the tax. Few assessments were made under this act. However, two which do survive are now available in print, and may enable you to identify ancestors:

- Ralph, Elizabeth, and Williams, Mary E., eds. *The Inhabitants of Bristol in 1696*. (Bristol Record Society publications 26, 1968).
- Glass, D.V., ed. *London Inhabitants within the Walls 1695*. (London Record Society 2, 1966).

In the early eighteenth century, parish registers continued to be kept. However, the period saw a rapidly increasing number of irregular and clandestine marriages, which had a deleterious effect on the keeping of parish registers. It meant that they failed to record an increasing proportion of the marriages which actually took place. Clandestine marriage records will be discussed in the next chapter.

Lord Hardwicke's Marriage Act of 1753 invalidated clandestine and irregular marriages. It required all marriages, except those of Jews and Quakers, to be conducted by Anglican clergymen (thus annoying Roman Catholics and Nonconformists). A valid marriage required either the calling of banns on three successive Sundays, or a licence from the bishop. The Act made important changes to the way in which marriage registers were kept. Henceforth, marriages had to be recorded in a prescribed format, on a printed form. Post-1753 marriage registers give the names and parish(es) of the parties, the date and place of marriage, whether by banns or licence, whether with the consent of parents or guardians, the name of the officiating minister, and the signatures of the parties, witnesses and minister. They were kept much more carefully than had previously been the case.

1783 saw another attempt to introduce a levy on parish register entries. It again attracted much opposition; one clergyman thought it 'a tax much vexatious to the clergy'.[9] It did, however, result in one innovation: printed registers for baptisms and burials, designed to enable the tax due to be easily calculated, were published, and in a few parishes new registers were commenced in 1783 in conse-

The fifteenth-century porch at St Buryan (Cornwall). Marriages would have been conducted here.

quence.[10] Paupers were exempt, and register entries are sometimes annotated with the letter 'P' to indicate paupers, or perhaps 'EP' to indicate 'exempt pauper'. The number of paupers naturally rose, and the number of babies being brought for baptism again declined. The levy was repealed in 1794. Children baptised after the repeal of the act may have been those who had not been brought for baptism whilst it was in force.

Meanwhile, William Dade, a Yorkshire clergyman, was pioneering a new form of marriage entry in parish registers. His practice was to include the occupations, statuses and ages of both parties. In 1777, Archbishop Markham approved Dade's proposed format, and ordered that it should be used throughout the Diocese of York. Dade registers, as they are known, are also widely found in other Northern dioceses, especially Chester and Durham.

Baptism and burial registers were finally brought into line with marriage registers when the use of printed forms for them was mandated by Rose's Act of 1812. The legislation took effect on 1 January 1813. Baptismal entries were to include the date of baptism, the name of the child, the names of parents, their abode, 'quality, trade or profession' and the name of the celebrant. Burial entries included the name of the deceased, his abode, his age, the date of burial and the name of the clergyman.

This legislation came into force as the number of baptisms recorded was steadily declining. The Church of England was losing out to the forces of Nonconformity and industrialization. In Chapter 1, we saw that the number of Nonconformists steadily increased during the late eighteenth and early nineteenth centuries. Most Nonconformists (some Methodists excepted) did not bring their babies to their Church of England clergyman to be baptised, and therefore their baptisms were not registered. By 1851, roughly a half of church attenders were attending non-Anglican places of worship.

At the same time, the urban working class was growing rapidly, overwhelming the church's ability to cope. Many failed to bring their babies for baptism. Nonconformity and urbanization together meant that births were not recorded. Parish registers were increasingly incapable of performing their function in the inheritance system.

The remedy devised by Parliament for this situation was to re-introduce civil registration. Births (not baptisms), and deaths (not burials) were to be registered by District Registrars, who were to send copies of their registers to the Registrar General every quarter. They were also to register marriages which did not take place in Anglican churches.

Civil registration did not affect parish baptism and burial registers. These continued (and continue) to be maintained. Marriages were treated differently, however. Henceforth, the clergy were required to compile duplicate marriage registers. One copy was to be retained by the church, the other sent to the District Registrar on completion (which could be many years after the first entry was made). In addition, the clergy were required to make quarterly returns of marriages to the Registrar General. These were copied into the General Register Office's registers, and then (presumably) destroyed. Hence there are three places in which Church of England marriages can be traced after 1837: the parish register, the register held by District Registrars, and the General Register Office's register (which, as just stated, is a copy of a copy, and therefore less good evidence than the other two registers). Entries in all three of these sources should in principle be identical. In practice, errors do creep in. Also, if amendments were made in the parish register after the other copies were made, that may not be reflected in them. In cases of doubt, it is best to check all copies of the entry.

The information in civil marriage registers include the place of marriage, the date of marriage, names and surnames of the parties, their ages, marital status, rank or profession, residence at the time of marriage, their fathers' names and professions, whether the marriage was by banns, licence, or registrar's certificate, and the signatures of the parties, witnesses and the celebrant.

There has been little change in the information recorded in baptism and burial parish registers since 1837. However, the number of entries made in them has gradually decreased in proportion to the population. As we have seen, Anglicanism in the second half of the twentieth century underwent a dramatic decline in numbers. Parish registers do, however, provide the information necessary to trace the baptisms, marriages and burials of all Anglicans.

Locating Parish Registers
Parish registers, and especially marriage registers, are normally deposited in local record offices when filled up, or when they have been in use for a century or more. Those still in use are normally kept in church safes, with access through the priest in charge. The county volumes of the *National Index of Parish Registers*, published by the Society of Genealogists, provide detailed listings of the location of all registers and copy registers. Record Office websites usually list the registers held. Many original registers can only be consulted on microfilm, or perhaps as digitized images. A summary listing covering the whole country is provided by:

• Humphery-Smith, Cecil. *The Phillimore Atlas and Index of Parish Registers*. (3rd ed. Phillimore, 2003).

B. PARISH REGISTER TRANSCRIPTS
Innumerable transcripts of parish registers are available, in manuscript, in print, and on the internet. Transcribers frequently deposited copies of their work with their local studies library, their local family history society and with the Society of Genealogists.

Many registers have been printed. The *Phillimore Parish Registers: Marriages* series includes transcripts of no less than 1,400 registers. There are or have been societies solely dedicated to publishing parish registers in a number of counties; those societies covering Lancashire, Shropshire, Staffordshire and Yorkshire have been particularly prolific. For London, many have been published by the Parish Register Section of the Harleian Society. Bedfordshire County Council has published all pre-1837 Bedfordshire registers (now available on CD from Bedfordshire Family History Society). Parish registers have also been published by some county record societies;

the Devon and Cornwall Record Society was particularly active in this regard before the Second World War. The Parish Register Society published over a hundred registers from a variety of counties in the late nineteenth and early twentieth centuries. More recently, many have been published by local family history societies, sometimes on CD or microfiche rather than in print; the societies for Birmingham and the Midlands, Kent and Wiltshire have been particularly active. Published registers are listed in Raymond's series of county genealogical bibliographies (see above, pp.55–6), although many have been issued since these were compiled.

C. PARISH REGISTERS ON THE INTERNET

More recently, numerous transcripts have appeared on the internet. They can frequently be identified through Genuki **www. genuki.org.uk**, and can usually also be found through general search engines such as Google **www.google.co.uk**. The Parish Register Transcription Society **https://www.parishchest.com/ Parish_Register_Transcription_Society_LID2318** has published transcripts for many counties. Many printed registers have been digitized, especially volumes from the Phillimore series. Commercial hosts (see above, p.60) have many transcripts on their databases, even if they sometimes fail to make clear the differences between transcripts, indexes, and digitized images.

Numerous digitized images of original parish registers are available on the internet. Family Search **https://familysearch.org** has an extensive collection from a variety of counties.

In North-West Kent, Medway Archives **http://cityark.medway. gov.uk** have digitized all their parish registers. Others have preferred to delegate the responsibility to commercial hosts. Registers from London Metropolitan Archives, for example, are available at Ancestry **www.ancestry.co.uk**. No doubt many more parish registers will be digitized by the time you read this book.

D. PARISH REGISTER INDEXES

Most transcripts and digitized images on the internet are supplied with their own indexes. However, there are numerous more general indexes available. The most important of these is the *International Genealogical Index*, popularly known as the *IGI* **https://family search.org/search/collection/igi**. This indexes microfilmed registers held by the Latter Day Saints' Family History Library, which can be consulted through its world-wide network of Family History Centres. Its coverage, as indicated by its title, is international. If you consult the microfilm, be sure that you check the status of any document that has been microfilmed. It may be the original register, but, equally, it may merely be a printed or manuscript transcript, in which case its evidential value will be less.

The *IGI* only covers baptisms and marriages. For deaths, wide coverage is provided by the National Burial Index. Some of this index is available through Find My Past **www.findmypast.co.uk** – but not all. The whole index is available on CD from the Federation of Family History Societies **www.ffhs.org.uk/projects/nbi**.

These are the most comprehensive indexes available, but their coverage is far from being complete. When you use them, always check whether the particular registers you are interested in have been indexed. Other major indexes include Boyd's Marriage index **www.societyofgenealogists.com/?s=boyd%27s+marriage+index** (now available on Genes Reunited **www.genesreunited.co.uk**), Pallot's Index 1780–1837 **http://search.ancestry.co.uk/search/ db.aspx?dbid=5967**, and the Joiner Marriage Index **http://joiner marriageindex.co.uk**. Numerous online and offline marriage indexes are listed in:

- Gibson, Jeremy, Hampson, Elizabeth, and Raymond, Stuart A. *Marriage Indexes for Family Historians.* (9th ed. Family History Partnership, 2008).

The warning given above (p.63) is pertinent here. It is important to appreciate that these indexes are just that: indexes. They are intended to enable you to locate entries in original parish registers, and are important for that purpose. They are NOT the original parish registers, and sometimes do not even index the original: they may be based on manuscript or printed transcripts, or perhaps on the bishops' transcripts. They do not necessarily provide you with all the information to be found in the original, or, indeed, in transcripts. For example, occupations and ages may be excluded. Always check original documents, rather than just relying on indexes. And if a digitized version of the original register can be found, that is much to be preferred to any transcript. It should provide you with an exact reproduction – although, again, heed the warning given above!

E. AFTERWORD

Sadly, many parish registers have been lost. As a general rule, the further back you go, the less likely are you to find them. Nevertheless, there are alternatives. These will be dealt with in the next chapter.

For a detailed and reasonably up-to-date guide to parish registers and their uses, see:

• Raymond, Stuart A. *Parish Registers: a History and Guide*. (Family History Partnership, 2009).

The classic text is:

• Steel, D.J. *National Index of Parish Registers, volume 1. Sources of births, marriages and deaths before 1837 (1)*. (Society of Genealogists, 1968).

Older texts, but still useful, include:

• Burn, John Southerden. *Parish Registers in England*. (2nd ed. John Russell Smith, 1862).
• Cox, J. Charles. *The Parish Registers of England*. (Methuen, 1910. Reprinted EP Publishing, 1974.)

- Waters, R.E. Chester. *Parish Registers in England*. (Longmans, Green & Co., 1897. Reprinted Family History Society of Cheshire, 1999).

Dade registers are discussed by:

- Bellingham, Roger. 'The Dade parish registers', *Family History News and Digest*, 10(2) (1995), pp.76–9.
- Bellingham, Roger. 'Dade registers', *Archives* 27(107) (2002), pp.134–47.
- Bellingham, Roger. 'Dade parish registers', *Local Population Studies* 73 (2004), pp.51–60. Available online at **www.localpopulationstudies.org.uk/journal.htm**

A detailed social history of the rituals associated with births, marriages and deaths in England is provided by:

- Cressy, David. *Birth, Marriage and Death: Ritual, Religion and the Life-Cycle in Tudor and Stuart England*. (Oxford University Press, 1997).

Chapter 5

OTHER SOURCES OF ANGLICAN BAPTISMS, MARRIAGES AND BURIALS

A. BISHOPS' TRANSCRIPTS

The canons of 1597 and 1603 required clergy to make transcripts of parish registers for their bishops annually, covering the year to 25 March. In most dioceses, they survive from then until the mid-nineteenth century, and occasionally later, although many have been lost. There are few for Essex, prior to 1800. Conversely, for the Diocese of Canterbury and the Archdeaconry of Lincoln, they survive from 1561. Few were compiled during the Civil War and Interregnum (1642–60), when episcopal governance was in abeyance. In many peculiars, no transcripts were made until legislation in 1812.

If bishops' transcripts are available, they should always be compared with original parish registers if possible. Although they were supposed to be identical, that was not necessarily the case. Some are heavily abbreviated, others offer more information than is given in the register.

Bishops' transcripts are found amongst diocesan records. For a national listing, see:

• Gibson, Jeremy. *Bishops' Transcripts and Marriage Licences, Bonds and Allegations: a Guide to their Location and Indexes.* (6th ed. Family History Partnership, 2013).

A detailed listing, parish by parish, is provided in the county volumes of the Society of Genealogists' *National Index of Parish Registers*. Record Office websites may list their holdings. Parish pages on Genuki **www.genuki.org.uk** also frequently indicate availability.

B. BANNS REGISTERS

Banns are public proclamations of intended marriages. Their purpose was (and is) to prevent invalid marriages taking place, by enabling anyone to point out impediments to the marriage. They have been regularly called in the parish church(es) of both parties to a marriage since 1215. Canons of 1575 required that congregations be 'openly asked' if they knew of any impediment to a marriage. After 1753, the requirement to call them on three successive Sundays could only be circumvented by obtaining a licence from the bishop.

During the Interregnum the practice of recording banns in parish registers was introduced, and very occasionally continued after the Restoration. From 1753, registers were again required; they had to be kept in books of printed forms. Surviving post-1753 printed registers are of three kinds: banns only, banns and marriages in separate halves of the same volume, and banns and marriages on the same form. Some registers were commenced after the Marriage Act of 1824, when it was laid down that 'the banns shall be published from the said register book of banns by the officiating minister, and not from loose papers, and after publication shall be signed by the officiating minister or by some person under his direction'.[1] From 1837, banns registers entirely separate from the marriage registers have been kept. In order to request a reading of the banns, each party had to submit a written notification of their intention to marry. Very detailed affidavits had to be submitted between 1 September 1822 and March 1823. Very occasionally, these notifications and affidavits survive, and may provide additional information.[2] After 1834, it became possible to substitute a registrar's certificate for the publication of banns. Such certificates rarely survive amongst parish records.

If the spouses lived in different parishes, banns should be recorded in the registers of both parishes. Both entries should record where the marriage was to take place, so you should be able to trace the home parishes of both parties. It may also be useful to compare entries in banns registers with those in marriage registers, as additional or different information may be provided.

Banns registers do not prove that marriages actually took place. Engagements could be broken off. Banns could be challenged. An entry in a marriage register is normally required to prove the fact of marriage.

C. MARRIAGE LICENCE RECORDS
The need for banns to be called could be circumvented by obtaining a marriage licence. They had been granted in the medieval period, but became much commoner from the sixteenth century onwards. Medieval licences sometimes required banns to be called once or twice, rather than three times; they could also grant permission for marriages to take place in a season when they would otherwise be forbidden, such as Lent. Post-Reformation licences circumvented the calling of banns altogether. However, the canons specified that marriage should only take place in the parish of one of the parties. This provision should have been included in ordinary marriage licences, although frequently it was not. Strict legality required a special licence from an archbishop in order to marry away from home.

Marriage licences were sometimes regarded as status symbols; they were more expensive than banns. Some gentlemen disliked the idea of having their intentions announced to all and sundry; they preferred to obtain a licence. Nonconformists wanted nothing to do with Church of England services; between 1754 and 1837, they frequently sought a licence rather than having banns read.

Licences were granted by bishops and their surrogates, by some archdeacons, and by some who held jurisdiction in peculiars. The Vicar General granted marriage licences on behalf of the Archbishop of Canterbury. Their issuing was a profitable sideline for the officials who granted them. It was in their interests to ignore the canonical requirements for a grant, and to issue licences when they should not have done. The number of licences granted fell substantially when Lord Hardwicke's Marriage Act of 1753 tightened up procedures.[3]

The marriage licence was given to the couple to be presented to the officiating clergyman. Very occasionally, the latter retained and filed it in the parish chest; consequently, licences can occasionally be found amongst parish records. Normally, however, it is necessary to consult diocesan records to trace grants of licences. Four distinct sources may survive: the allegation, the bond, the register, and (in 1822–3 only) the affidavit.

Application for a marriage licence was made by submitting an allegation, that is, a sworn statement that there was no impediment to the marriage. Allegations gave the names of the parties, their ages (which should be treated cautiously), their places of abode, their status or occupations, and, if one of the parties was a minor, the name of a consenting parent or guardian.

Between 1597 and 1823, an allegation had to be accompanied by a bond, entered into by two bondsmen. It indemnified the official granting the licence if any of the conditions contained in the licence were not met. The conditions were that there was no impediment to the marriage, that any parental consent needed had been granted, and (from 1604), that the marriage would take place in a church where one of the parties lived.

Until 1733, the first part of the bond was in Latin. The bondsmen generally included the groom. By the eighteenth century, the second bondsman was frequently fictitious; in Surrey, after 1770, one of the bondsmen was always John Doe. Bonds for minors might be annotated by the parent(s) to indicate consent.

Registers of licences issued, or account books of licence fees received, were kept in some dioceses. For a very short space of time, between 1 September 1822 and 31 March 1823, affidavits stating the names, ages, and marital status of both parties had to be sworn when a licence was requested. If one of the parties was a minor, the written and witnessed consent of a parent was also required. Ages were proved by providing baptismal certificate.

Usually, at least one of these sources survives, sometimes several. Check them all: their details may differ. Licensing authority jurisdictions sometimes overlapped, so it may be necessary to search the records of two or three different jurisdictions. Licences were valid for three months, so, if you find evidence of a licence, you will need to search registers for three months from the date of its issue. Licence records identify the church in which a marriage was to take place, but there were occasions when it actually took place elsewhere. As in the case of banns, the fact that a licence was issued does not prove that the marriage took place.

For a detailed guide to marriage licences, visit:

• Lambeth Palace Library Research Guide: Marriage Records
  www.lambethpalacelibrary.org/files/marriage_records_0.pdf

Lambeth Palace Library holds the licensing records of the Vicar General of the Archbishop of Canterbury, and of the Faculty Office, both of which had jurisdiction over the whole of the Southern Province (The Archdiocese of Canterbury). For an index to the Vicar General's records, 1694–1850, visit:

• Vicar General Marriage Licences:
  http://search.findmypast.com/search-world-records/vicar-general-marriage-licences
  This page also has a link to an index to Faculty Office allegations from 1533 (see also below, pp.139–40).

For an index to bonds and allegations in the Northern Province, and especially in the Diocese of York, see:

• Yorkshire, Archbishop of York Marriage Licences: Index, 1613–1839
  http://search.findmypast.com/search-world-records/yorkshire-archbishop-of-york-marriage-licences-index-1613-1839

Numerous abstracts and indexes of marriage licence records from individual dioceses are also available, in manuscript, print, and occasionally online. For a detailed listing (including details of printed indexes to the Provincial records mentioned above), see:

- Gibson, Jeremy. *Bishops' Transcripts and Marriage Licences, Bonds and Allegations: a Guide to their Location and Indexes.* (6th ed. Family History Partnership, 2013).

D. IRREGULAR AND CLANDESTINE MARRIAGES

Marriage had not originally been a matter for the church. Under the common law, a valid marriage merely required the consent of both parties made before witnesses. By the sixteenth century, however, it had become almost a universal custom to be married at the church door. But the requirements of the canon law outlined above were increasingly being disregarded at the end of the seventeenth century. Marriages conducted without banns or licence were invalid in the eyes of the church; those who married in this way were sometimes hauled before the ecclesiastical courts, and could be excommunicated (see pp.123–5). Such marriages were, however, valid at common law, and were cheaper than marriage by licence. Consequently, irregular and clandestine marriages, conducted in accordance with the common law, became increasingly common. They were conducted in peculiars outside of the jurisdiction of diocesan bishops, where the priests who conducted them were not in danger of ecclesiastical censure. Some priests were able to establish lucrative 'marriage centres', where irregular or clandestine marriages could be conducted for a small fee. Most counties had such centres; those which are best known were in London: Holy Trinity, Minories, St James's, Dukes Place, and St. Botolph's, Aldgate. There were no less than 1,803 marriages at Duke's Place in 1690 alone.[4]

In 1695, legislation stamped out most of this trade in peculiars. It did not, however, abolish common law marriage. The trade was merely displaced to places where bishops continued to lack jurisdiction, especially in the Liberty of the Fleet. The Fleet was a debtors' prison, and there were always priests amongst the debtors willing to conduct marriages for a fee. By the middle of the eighteenth century, perhaps half of all London marriages were being conducted irregularly, in the Fleet. The celebrants kept their own registers, some of which are now in the National Archives, class RG 7,[5] and have been digitized at:

- BMD Registers
  www.bmdregisters.co.uk

Irregular and clandestine marriage was thought to nullify parental authority, to threaten the inheritance of property, and to deprive parochial incumbents of a legitimate source of their income. It was not until 1753 that Lord Hardwicke's Marriage Act put a stop to the practice. It abolished common law marriage, requiring all marriages, except those of Jews and Quakers, to be conducted by an Anglican priest.

Further Reading
For a general study of clandestine marriage, with a transcript of Lord Hardwicke's 1753 Marriage Act, see:

- Outhwaite, R.B. *Clandestine Marriage in England 1500-1850.* (Hambledown Press, 1995).

Sources for genealogists are discussed in:

- Benton, Tony. *Irregular Marriages in London before 1754.* (2nd ed. Society of Genealogists, 2000).

E. BAPTISMAL CERTIFICATES
In the eighteenth and nineteenth centuries, increasing numbers of people needed to prove their ages, especially if they sought appointments in the civil service or the armed forces. Men seeking

ordination had to prove their ages to the bishop. Those born before the introduction of civil registration in 1837 could do so by obtaining a baptismal certificate. In 1822–3, as mentioned above, these had to be produced to prove ages when marriage licences were sought. Certificates were issued by parish priests on request.

These certificates were given to individuals to use for a variety of different purposes, and may sometimes be found amongst family and estate papers. They survive in a number of National Archives classes. Baptismal certificates for army officers 1755–1908 may be found in WO 42, and for 1777–1868 in WO 32/8903-20. Royal Naval officers' passing certificates frequently have baptismal certificates attached; these are in ADM 6, ADM 13 and ADM 107. Civil Service evidences of age, which include baptismal certificates, are held by the Society of Genealogists, and are indexed online at **www.findmy past.co.uk/articles** (click 'Full List of United Kingdom Records', and scroll down to title). Certificates produced to bishops can be found amongst ordination papers in Diocesan archives.

F. MONUMENTAL INSCRIPTIONS

Memorials to the dead are found in most churches and churchyards. Sixteenth- and seventeenth-century gentry were frequently memorialized. In the eighteenth century the practice gradually became more widespread. Some of your nineteenth- and twentieth-century ancestors have probably been remembered in this way. Churchyards are full of memorials of the lower classes. War memorials are frequently found. Memorials of the gentry and aristocracy are more likely to be inside the church; so are memorials of at least some incumbents.

There is no standard format for memorial inscriptions. Some merely give a name and the date of death. Others add ages, occupations, and places of origin. The deceased may be eulogized in verse. Many gravestones quote Biblical verses. Sometimes entire families are commemorated on one gravestone, or indeed on a whole series of gravestones placed closely together.

Memorial for a Somerset rector – Thomas Leir of Ditcheat.

Locating memorials is not necessarily easy, especially in view of the fact that places of burial are not mentioned on GRO certificates. Many have been transcribed by family history societies and others. Transcripts are frequently made in triplicate, with one copy held by the relevant local studies library, one by the local family history society, and one deposited at the Society of Genealogists. Family history societies have published many inscriptions; details can be found on their websites. Published monumental inscriptions are also listed in the county volumes of Raymond's series of British genealogical library guides (see above, pp.55–6). Numerous transcripts

The mainly fifteenth-century church at Church Hanborough in Oxfordshire, with its graveyard.

and photographs of inscriptions are also available on internet sites. For an attempt to provide a directory of such sites, see:

- Tombstones & Monumental Inscriptions
www.burial-inscriptions.co.uk

For war memorials, see:

- Tall, Susan. *War Memorials: a Guide for Family Historians.* (Family History Partnership, 2014).

G. OTHER SOURCES

Churchwardens' accounts, which record receipts for various fees incurred at funerals, and parish magazines, which may contain extracts from the parish registers, are discussed in the following chapter. A variety of others sources for baptisms/births, marriages, and deaths/burials, are discussed in:

- Raymond, Stuart A. *Vital Records for Family Historians.* (3 vols. Family History Partnership, 2010–11). Vol. 1. *Birth and Baptism Records for Family Historians.* Vol. 2. *Marriage Records for Family Historians.* Vol. 3. *Death and Burial Records for Family Historians.*

Chapter 6

OTHER PARISH RECORDS

A wide variety of documents were formerly stored in parish chests. We have already considered parish registers and associated documents. Most of the other records were created by parish officers: churchwardens, overseers of the poor, parish constables and highway surveyors. A few were written by incumbents. Not all the documents in parish chests dealt with ecclesiastical matters. The Tudors and Stuarts had adapted the mechanisms of ecclesiastical government for secular purposes, and matters such as the poor law, the repair of roads, and the maintenance of the law came within the purview of parish government as much as more purely ecclesiastical matters. This book is concerned with tracing Anglican ancestors, so only the strictly ecclesiastical sources will be considered here.

A. CHURCHWARDENS' ACCOUNTS AND ASSOCIATED RECORDS
The role of churchwardens was discussed in Chapter 2. Their accounts provide vivid details of parish life, and provide us with much information about our ancestors. They record how parishes raised money, and how it was spent. After the Reformation, church rates were frequently levied on householders. Lists of ratepayers are therefore likely to be found in churchwardens' accounts, or may sometimes be found separately. A run of ratepayers' lists may enable the genealogist to date an ancestor's presence in a particular parish. Income was also raised from parish property, especially in cities, where wealthy testators sometimes bequeathed lands and houses to parishes. Accounts may mention the names of tenants. Social events were also used to raise money, although these were less

frequent in the late sixteenth and seventeenth centuries than they were before or since. Puritan sensibilities in that era frequently raised objections to conducting 'church ales', Robin Hood plays or dances. Since the late nineteenth century, it has become the custom to take a collection during church services; purchases of collection plates and bags may be recorded in accounts.

Subscriptions could be invited for major expenses, such as installing an organ, building a gallery or building a new church. Major contributions might be made by the local landowner. In the nineteenth century, subscriptions gradually came to replace compulsory rates as a means of raising money. The latter became increasingly controversial amongst Nonconformists and other non-churchgoers, and ceased to be worth the trouble they caused. In 1845, the incumbent of Princes Risborough commented that 'if an attempt were made to levy a rate for the repairs of the steeple, an angry spirit would be stirred up productive of much evil'; in contrast, if the proposed subscription were successful it might 'bring some back to the church', or at least 'diminish the bitter feeling some of the Dissenters entertain'.[1] Many lists of subscribers can be found in accounts, or amongst other parish records, enabling us to identify ancestors who contributed. Incidentally, the religious orders discussed in Chapter 9 also relied on subscribers.

Louth in Lincolnshire – the tallest parish church spire in England, built by the churchwardens.

The guildhouse at Poundstock in Cornwall – the responsibility of the churchwardens.

Churchwardens also raised money from parishioners' deaths. Payments for grave digging, ringing the knells and the hire of the parish bier are frequently recorded in some accounts, so much so that on occasion accounts can be used as a substitute for registers of burials.

The money raised was used for a variety of purposes. The prime responsibility of churchwardens was the fabric of the church. Accounts frequently record payments to tradesmen such as masons, plumbers, glaziers and carpenters. If you are searching for such tradesmen, it may be worth consulting accounts for neighbouring parishes. Those who undertook such work in one parish were likely to work in neighbouring parishes as well.

Churchwardens also provided communion bread and wine, so their accounts may indicate the regularity with which communion services were held. Accounts may record the purchase of bibles, prayer books, hymnals and musical instruments. Parish servants such as organists, gravediggers and even dog-whippers had to be paid, so their names are likely to be recorded. The role of churchwardens as dispensers of charity was also important; many, for example, paid for sufferers from the King's Evil (scrofula) to travel for the purpose of obtaining the King's touch, which was thought to cure them. Sufferers' names may be recorded in accounts, or perhaps in registers of the certificates which had to be issued in order to obtain access to the royal presence.[2] Another responsibility of the church-wardens was to represent the parish at ecclesiastical visitations. They claimed their expenses for doing so, and their attendance was therefore recorded in their accounts.

Many churchwardens' accounts record the activities of other parish officers: overseers, highway surveyors, and constables. Hence the names of paupers who received relief, of offenders escorted to Quarter Sessions by constables, and of those who met their obligation to work on the roads by monetary payment, may be recorded.

Many churchwardens' accounts are in print. See, for example:

- Hanham, Alison, ed. *Churchwardens' Accounts of Ashburton, 1479-1580.* (Devon & Cornwall Record Society new series 15. 1970).
- Ramsay, Esther M.E., and Maddock, Alison J., eds. *The Churchwardens Accounts of Walton -on-the-Hill, Lancashire, 1627-1667.* (Record Society of Lancashire and Cheshire, 141. 2005).

London churchwardens' accounts are listed in:

- *Churchwardens' Accounts of Parishes within the City of London: a Handlist.* (2nd ed. Guildhall Library, 1960).

The classic discussion of churchwardens' accounts is provided by:

- Cox, J. Charles. *Churchwardens' Accounts from the Fourteenth Century to the Close of the Seventeenth Century.* (Methuen & Co., 1913).

For a recent collection of essays, see:

• Hitchman, Valerie, and Foster, Andrew, eds. *Views from the Parish: Churchwardens' Accounts, c.1500-c.1800.* (Cambridge Scholars Publishing, 2015).

B. VESTRY MINUTES

The vestry was the forum in which matters relating to parish government were settled. It appointed one of the churchwardens, and nominated other parish officers. It dealt with a wide range of both ecclesiastical and secular matters. Roads, church fabric and vermin were all within its purview. After 1850, many vestries were responsible for erecting village halls. As vestry activities increased, bureaucracy crept in. From the eighteenth century onwards, vestries in larger parishes sometimes appointed their own clerks to keep minutes and deal with vestry affairs on a day-to-day basis.

The composition of vestries varied from parish to parish. In some places, they were open to all householders. Elsewhere, they could be self-selecting oligarchies, composed of the most substantial men in the parish. Originally, they met in church. In the Victorian era, however, it was frequently held that churches should only be used for divine worship; even the vestry had to meet elsewhere.

Most surviving vestry minutes date from the eighteenth and nineteenth centuries. Earlier decisions are frequently recorded in churchwardens' accounts. Minutes are likely to give the date and place of each meeting, together with the names of those in attendance. They record specific decisions, such as the setting of rates or the installation of an organ. Nominations of officers were made annually, and recorded. Appointments of parish servants such as organists, vergers and parish clerks are likely to be minuted.

For a good example of vestry minutes in print, see:

• Cowe, F.M., ed. *Wimbledon Vestry Minutes 1736, 1743-1788: a Calendar.* (Surrey Record Society 25. 1964).

London vestry minutes are listed by:

• *Vestry Minutes of Parishes within the City of London* . . . . (2nd ed. Guildhall Library, 1960).

C. SEATING PLANS
In the medieval period there were frequently no seats in church. Services did not require them, congregations moved about freely in the nave, and pews might have blocked the way for processions. They began to be introduced in the fourteenth and fifteenth centuries. After the Reformation, the shift of emphasis from the celebration of the Eucharist to the hearing of sermons, combined with increased congregational participation in services, meant that worshippers needed to sit down.[3] Indeed, the *Book of Common Prayer* specified when the congregation was to stand, and when to sit.

In an age when everyone attended church, and when social status was regarded as being of the utmost importance, seating arrangements in church mattered. The introduction of pews meant the end of the free-for-all of an open church, and the introduction of order based on hierarchy, social status, wealth and prestige. When the vestry of Kingston upon Thames decided to alter seating arrangements in 1585, they ordered 'the parishioners to be placed in order in their degrees and callinges'.[4] Those at the top of the pinnacle took a proprietorial attitude towards their pews, perhaps marking them with their names on brass plates, or with heraldic arms. In many places, the right to a particular pew could be bought and sold. Jesus's injunction to take the lower seat was frequently ignored. More positively, possession of a fixed seat in church could engender a sense of community, help to make the church the centre of that community and enhance worship. Even in 1914, about one in six seats were appropriated to private use, although the practice of selling them had virtually died out.

Generally, the manorial lord, the leading gentry and yeomen, and the family of the incumbent sat towards the front. Husbandmen (smallholders) and tradesmen sat behind them, labourers towards the back and paupers were allocated benches at the back. At St Edmunds, Salisbury, benches were ordered to be labelled 'for the poore' in 1628. Paupers had to sit there; their poor relief might be withdrawn if they were absent. By contrast, manorial lords sometimes occupied a whole transept, as the Hoare family did at Stourton in Wiltshire. The Hoares even had their own fireplace!

Bishops supervised seating arrangements. They delegated their authority to churchwardens. Theirs was an invidious task, which could easily involve them in disputes before the ecclesiastical courts (see pp.116–31), especially when two householders claimed the same seat.

The fireplace in the Hoare pew at Stourton in Wiltshire.

Decisions about seating arrangements therefore had to be carefully made. Many churchwardens drew up seating plans, showing where parishioners were to sit. These are likely to list all heads of households, and are virtually censuses of parish families. They reveal the pecking order in the community. Some church-wardens were indignant at being deprived of their authority over pews when, in the early nineteenth century, the Incorporated Church Building Society insisted that pews supported by its funding should be free.[5] Seating plans were especially necessary when new pews were installed. Occasionally, several plans for the same parish survive, enabling detailed study of changes in social structure.

Other references to seating frequently occur in parish records. The parish register of Corsham (Wiltshire) includes numerous memoranda concerning pews and their owners. For example, on 20 September 1720 'the seat adjoining the first pillar on the right hand of the west door was repaired at the expense of Mr Jonathan Rogers'.[6] Another example is provided by the churchwardens' accounts of Ashburton (Devon), which, in 1527–8, records the receipt of four shillings 'for seats sold in the church'. The purchasers are named.[7]

For pews in general, see:

• Cooper, Trevor, and Brown, Sarah, eds. *Pews, Benches & Chairs: Church Seating in English Parish Churches from the Fourteenth Century to the Present*. (Ecclesiological Society, 2011).

Seating plans are discussed by:

• Thomas, Spencer. 'Pews their Setting, Symbolism, and Significance', *Local Historian* 39(4) (2009), pp.267–86. Available online at **www.balh.org.uk/publications/local-historian**

A lawyer's collection of some 1,400 documents relating to church pews from the seventeenth century and earlier is printed in:

- Heales, Alfred. *The History and Law of Church Seats or Pews*. (Butterworths, 1872).

One of the earliest parish histories ever written (1700) was based on a seating plan. For a modern edition, see:

- Gough, Richard. *The History of Myddle*, with introduction by Peter Razzle. (Caliban Books, 1979). Originally entitled *Antiquities and Memoirs of the Parish of Myddle*. There are several other editions.

D. TITHE RECORDS

Tithing – the practice of giving a tenth of one's income to the church – is a biblical principle. Tithes were made compulsory in England under the Anglo-Saxon monarchs, and lasted, with modifications, until the early twentieth century. The idea that giving should be voluntary did not occur to our ancestors.

There was a basic legal distinction between 'personal' and 'predial' tithes. Personal tithes were supposed to be paid on their incomes by wage and salary earners, craftsmen and merchants, after their expenses had been deducted. Predial tithes were levied on the produce of the earth, such as corn. Some sources of income, such as wool, cheese, milk and the young of animals, were regarded as 'mixed'. Expenses were not allowed in the assessment of the amounts due for predial and mixed tithes.

Most people in the sixteenth and seventeenth centuries were willing to pay tithes in return for the spiritual services of their local church. However, the linkage between tithes and the local church had been badly damaged by the Reformation. It was increasingly difficult to see the connection when tithes went to distant pluralists who never visited their parishes, or even to laymen (impropriators) whose ancestors had purchased the property of dissolved monasteries. Nonconformists were foremost in challenging the principle of tithes, which became increasingly contentious in the eighteenth century. In 1736, the Society of Friends claimed that their members had suffered no less than 1,180 tithe prosecutions since 1696.[8]

Tithing customs varied from parish to parish, but, by the eighteenth century, tithes had effectively become a tax on the agricultural interest. Unfortunately, as has already been noted, they also constituted an important part of clergy income. Tithes were difficult to assess and collect. Disputes concerning them could make it almost impossible for the clergy to provide the spiritual care for their parishioners which was their *raison d'être*. If a rector brought a test case against one of his parishioners, it was quite likely that others would be affected if he was successful.[9] Clergy sometimes avoided collecting them in person by leasing them for a fixed sum to a tithe farmer. Tithe farmers, together with lay impropriators, were probably responsible for the majority of tithe causes brought before the courts. Such litigation caused much ill feeling.

Many tithe cases came before the ecclesiastical courts (see Chapter 7) in the sixteenth and seventeenth centuries. Their tithe jurisdiction, however, became increasingly ineffective. The secular courts claimed jurisdiction over financial matters, and frequently prevented ecclesiastical courts hearing particular cases. Even in the late sixteenth century, 75 per cent of prohibitions issued by them against Consistory Courts related to tithes.[10] In 1696, Justices of the Peace were given additional powers over tithes, and the number of tithe cases coming before ecclesiastical courts slumped.[11] Most eighteenth-century tithe litigants sought judgement before royal judges in Chancery, or in one of the other Westminster courts.

As early as 1549, Kett's Norfolk rebels had demanded the commutation of tithes in kind for a monetary payment.[12] Three hundred years later, that solution to the problem was endorsed by the Tithe Commutation Act of 1836. The tithe maps and awards compiled in accordance with the Act are important sources for researchers, although they do not generally cover parishes where tithes had already been commuted during enclosure. Awards list the names of every landowner and tenant in the parish; the accompanying maps show where their lands lay. Three copies of these documents were kept: one was retained in the parish chest, one deposited with the Diocesan Registrar, and one was sent to the

Tithe Commissioners in London. These records are now usually to be found either in local record offices, or, in the case of the Tithe Commissioners' copies, in The National Archives, classes IR 29 (apportionments) and IR 30 (maps). The National Archives also hold tithe files (IR 18) containing the correspondence of the Tithe Commissioners with each parish.

Many other tithe records were kept in parish chests. Tithing customs and agreements were frequently written into parish registers, churchwardens' accounts, or ecclesiastical terriers. Incumbents sometimes kept their own accounts of what they had received. Tithe books may list every householder in the parish, and provide a great deal of information about them – not just the amounts they paid, but also details of their farms, perhaps their religious affiliations, and sometimes more personal observations. In some parishes, a fixed Easter offering was agreed as a substitute for personal tithes; these are discussed below. In others, mortuaries were paid when parishioners died. These were considered to provide recompense for tithes which had not been paid. Both could be mentioned in glebe terriers (see below, pp.112–13).

Further Reading
The authoritative guide to tithe maps and apportionments is provided by:

• Kain, Roger J.P., and Prince, Hugh C. *Tithe Surveys for Historians.* (Phillimore, 2000).

For more basic introductions, see:

• Evans, Eric J. *Tithes: Maps, Apportionments and the 1836 Act: a Guide for Local Historians.* (3rd ed. British Association for Local History, 1997).
• Beech, Geraldine, and Mitchell, Rose. *Maps for Family and Local History: the Records of the Tithe, Valuation Office and National Farm Surveys of England and Wales, 1836-1943.* (2nd ed. National Archives, 2004).

- How to Look for Records of Tithes
  www.nationalarchives.gov.uk/help-with-your-research/ research-guides/tithes/

For a brief introduction to pre-1836 tithe books, see:

- Evans, Nesta. 'Tithe books as a source for the local historian', *Local Historian* 14 (1980), pp.24–7.

For documentation of some of the innumerable tithe disputes that came before ecclesiastical courts, see:

- Purvis, J.S., ed. *Select Sixteenth Century Causes in Tithe from York, Diocesan Registry.* (Yorkshire Archaeological Society Record Series 114. 1949).

Eighteenth-century tithe accounts prepared by the rector of Datchworth are printed in:

- Walker, Jane, ed. *Datchworth Tithe Accounts, 1711-1747.* (Hertfordshire Record Society 25. 2009).

Apportionments arising from the 1836 Act are printed in:

- Walker, Peter L., ed. *Tithe Apportionments of Worcestershire, 1837-1851* (includes CD). (Worcestershire Historical Society new series 23. 2011).

For tithe files, see:

- Beckett, J.V., and Heath, J. eds. *Derbyshire Tithe Files, 1836-50.* (Derbyshire Record Society 22. 1995).

E. EASTER BOOKS
Tradesmen were supposed to pay tithes, but in a pre-literate age, with no written accounts, it was impossible to assess the amounts

due. Consequently, fixed Easter offerings were substituted. These are frequently mentioned in glebe terriers, and the actual amounts received are recorded in Easter books and rolls.

These documents effectively serve as censuses of the population, and their financial nature means they are likely to be more accurate than most other population listings. If several Easter books survive from the same parish, it may be possible to trace the movements of householders, and possibly also of servants, over several decades. Local historians could also use them to investigate local social structure. A full listing of surviving Easter books is included in the second part of:

• Wright, S.J., 'A Guide to Easter Books and Related parish Listings', *Local Population Studies* 42 (1988), pp.18–31; 43, 1989, pp.13–27. Digitized at **www.localpopulationstudies.org. uk/journal.htm**

F. CONFIRMATION REGISTERS

The rite of confirmation enabled teenagers and adults to confirm the baptismal promises godparents had made in their names. The names of those confirmed were rarely recorded, at least in the Church of England. Nevertheless, records can be found. Lists of confirmees in 1703 and 1711 were written into the parish register of Stourton (Wiltshire).[13] Other parish books might also be used. On very rare occasions, separate confirmation registers might be found. Nineteenth- and twentieth-century lists and registers are much more likely to be available than those from earlier centuries.

G. INCUMBENTS' VISITING BOOKS

Incumbents' visiting books were compiled in order to aid the clergy when visiting their parishioners, and may give as much information as the official nineteenth-century censuses. Detailed listings of such books are provided in:

• Chapman, Colin R. *Pre-1841 Censuses & Population Listings in the British Isles.* (5th ed. Lochin Publishing, 1998).

- Gibson, Jeremy, and Medlycott, Mervyn. *Local Census Listings, 1522-1930: holdings in the British Isles.* (3rd ed. Federation of Family History Societies, 1997).

A number for Wiltshire have been published:

- Hurley, Beryl, ed. *Incumbents' Visiting Books.* (Wiltshire Family History Society, 1994).

H. PARISH MAGAZINES

Since the late nineteenth century, energetic incumbents and their helpers have published church magazines. These contain a wide range of material: letters from the incumbent or the bishop, notices of forthcoming events, reports of meetings, details of baptisms, marriages and burials, and the names of those responsible for various activities, such as organists, youth club leaders, church-wardens and flower arrangers. Sometimes they were published in conjunction with diocesan magazines. They still are. They provide a great deal of information on parish life at the time they were issued, and provide much information on who was doing what. We can even use them as substitutes for the parish register!

Sadly, complete runs of parish magazines are only infrequently found. They have sometimes been deposited in local studies libraries, or in local record offices with other parish records. It is also worth checking in the church itself to see whether any issues have been kept. For a detailed discussion, see:

- Platt, Jane. *Subscribing to the Faith: the Anglican Parish Magazine 1859-1929.* (Palgrave Macmillan, 2015).

I. MISCELLANEOUS DOCUMENTS

A wide variety of other documents can be found amongst parish records. It is not necessarily easy to divide those which are primarily concerned with ecclesiastical matters from those of secular provenance. Deeds of church property may give the names of donors, churchwardens, etc. There may be records of certificates issued to sufferers from the King's Evil (scrofula); these were needed in order to gain admission to the royal presence. More recently, Sunday schools, youth clubs, the Mothers' Union, and other parish organizations have kept records of their activities. It is not possible to provide a comprehensive description of parish records; every parish is different.

Further Reading
For a detailed and up-to-date discussion of the contents of parish chests, both ecclesiastical and secular, see:

• Raymond, Stuart A. *Tracing your Ancestors' Parish Records: a Guide for Family and Local Historians.* (Pen & Sword, 2015).

A much older work (originally published in 1946), which obviously does not cover internet resources, but is nevertheless still valuable, is:

• Tate, W.E. *The Parish Chest: a Study of the Records of Parochial Administration in England.* (3rd ed., reprinted Phillimore, 2011).

Chapter 7

DIOCESAN, CHAPTER AND PROVINCIAL RECORDS

In my district once there used to be,
A fine Archdeacon, one of high degree,
Who bravely did the execution due,
On fornication, and on witchcraft too,
Bawdry, adultery and defamation,
Breaches of wills and contracts, spoliation,
Of church endowment, failure in church rents,
And tithes, and disregard of Sacraments.
All these, and certain other sorts of crime,
That need no mention at this time,
Like simony or usury, but he would boast,
That lechery was what he punished most.
They had to sing for it if they were caught,
Like those who failed to pay the tithes they ought.
As for all such, if there was an informant,
Nothing could save them from pecunial torment,
For those whose tithes and offerings were small,
Were made to sing the saddest song of all,
And ere the Bishop caught them with his crook,
Down they went in the Archdeacon's book,
For he had jurisdiction, after detection,
And power to administer correction.
                    Geoffrey Chaucer, *The Friar's Tale*[1]

A number of records kept by diocesan registrars have already been discussed: bishops' transcripts, marriage licences and glebe terriers.

Probate records will be discussed in Chapter 8. Clergy records will be discussed in Chapter 10. This chapter will deal with the records of ecclesiastical visitations and the church courts (other than probate), with the licences required by schoolmasters, surgeons, and midwives, and with the proofs of loyalty required by government from office-holders and others. Similar records were kept by cathedral chapters, and by the Archbishops. They also kept other records which will be discussed below. Some of these records were being kept long before the break with Rome. Despite that break, ecclesiastical administration saw minimal change in the sixteenth-century. Chaucer's fourteenth-century comments are just as applicable to seventeenth-century church courts and visitations as they were when he made them. The records of the Church Commissioners and their predecessors, will also be dealt with here.

For overviews of diocesan and provincial archives, see:

- Owen, Dorothy M. *Records of the Established Church in England excluding Parochial Records*. (Archives and the User 1. British Records Association, 1970).
- Purvis, J.S. *An Introduction to Ecclesiastical Records*. (St. Anthony's Press, 1953).

A. VISITATION RECORDS
Since the thirteenth century, bishops have conducted visitations of their dioceses every three or four years. Episcopal visitations were the 'keystone of the arch' of ecclesiastical administration,[2] usually conducted by the Chancellor or the Official of the Diocese. In the period between episcopal visitations, archdeacons conducted their own six-monthly visitations.

Visitations were normally held at a central place in each deanery. When their time and place had been decided, a general monition was issued to 'all parsons and vicars to exhibit letters of orders, certificates of subscriptions and dispensations, all preachers, lecturers, curates, readers, schoolmasters and ushers to exhibit licence, all impropriators and farmers to tithes to exhibit

Lincoln's medieval cathedral, seat of the bishop.

endowments and pay pensions and procurations, all churchmen and sidemen to take their oaths and make presentments, executors to bring in the wills of their testators, all criminals and delinquents to answer articles . . .'.

The Diocesan Registrar also prepared various books in advance of the visitation. Call books list the clergy and churchwardens who were summoned for the archdeacon's visitation, and record the amounts due for synodals, procurations and other dues. These are perhaps the most important source for identifying churchwardens.

The *liber cleri* identify the clergy, and sometimes schoolmasters, required to appear at episcopal visitations. They include memoranda relating to the rights of clergy to officiate, such as their orders, their licences, and their certificates of institution. Churchwardens' presentments were sometimes sent in before visitations commenced,[3]

The nineteenth-century cathedral at Truro.

and digests of them were made for the court. Alternatively, they might be presented orally, and written down by court officials. Citations were issued to those whose behaviour was thought to warrant consideration by the visitor. Any action taken was subsequently recorded in the digests.

Churchwardens' presentments reported on a wide range of matters. The fabric and furnishings of the church was a perennial topic, of direct concern to all churchwardens. The sins of parishioners – especially their sexual sins – were recorded. Drunkenness, misbehaviour in church and defamation were all frequently mentioned. So, until the end of the seventeenth century, was the absence from church of Nonconformists and Roman Catholics. Specific accusations were termed 'detections', and were sometimes gathered together in a volume of *detecta* or *comperta* at the end of visitations.

Churchwardens did not like presenting their neighbours, although they were legally obligated to do so. Late sixteenth-century visitation records are full of complaints that they had concealed offences or made inaccurate presentments. The courts sometimes interrogated churchwardens to verify their presentments; that is probably the reason why churchwardens from no less than seventeen parishes at the Archbishop of York's 1632–3 visitation were charged with neglecting to make true presentments.[4] The clergy, apparitors, and even informers could all report illegalities that churchwardens ignored. Perhaps the most accurate presentments were made after 1660, when churchwardens were enthusiastic about the Restoration settlement. Presentments for religious offences constituted half of the presentments made in the Peterborough court between 1662 and 1664.[5]

The enthusiasm of churchwardens was not to last. Presentments for religious reasons ceased after James II's Declaration of Indulgence in 1687, and the Toleration Act of 1689, both of which suspended the laws against non-attendance at church (although they did not actually repeal them). Increasingly, churchwardens failed to report the sins of their neighbours, despite the queries issued by bishops prior to visitation. Eighteenth-century presentments frequently record *omnia bene* – all well. All was, in fact, not always well – but the business the churchwardens were more likely to be concerned about, such as bastardy (which could cost the parish money for the maintenance of the bastard), was increasingly dealt with more efficiently by Justices of the Peace. Their numbers were steadily increasing, and they could issue bastardy bonds at any time, whereas the church courts were only available when they were sitting. By the end of the eighteenth century, charges concerning sexual offences had almost ceased to be heard in the ecclesiastical courts.[6] Churchwardens' presentments should not be taken as reliable indicators of the state of either the religious beliefs, or the moral behaviour, of parishioners between the sixteenth and the eighteenth centuries.

The response of the bishops to churchwardens' presentments of *omnia bene* was to issue articles of inquiry specifying the matters on which information was required. Presentments of the eighteenth and nineteenth centuries frequently reflect these queries, although still tending to avoid troublesome issues. As early as 1692, the Bishop of Lincoln was commissioning clergy in each deanery to report on church fabric. In 90 per cent of Leicestershire cases, churchwardens had reported *omnia bene*. The reports of the deanery clergy showed that in three-quarters of cases, there were issues which should have been presented.[7]

The bishops also directed queries to clergy. The earliest such queries were issued in the sixteenth century, became increasingly common after the Restoration, and were usually issued before bishops' primary visitations during the eighteenth century. These queries covered the whole range of topics in which bishops were interested: church fabric, ministry, and the conduct of parishioners. Questions were frequently asked about Nonconformity, schools, and charities. Bishops regarded the clergy as the best source of information on the state of their diocese. Replies to queries were sometimes collected together, to serve as surveys of the state of the diocese. Sometimes digests of them, known as *Specula*, were compiled; these might be annotated by the bishop himself during visitations. A number have been published, and are listed below.

Another document sometimes drawn up in advance of episcopal visitations was the glebe terrier. The glebe was the land given to the church for the use of parish incumbents, which became their freehold whilst they held office. A canon of 1571, renewed in 1603, required clergy to prepare terriers (the word is derived from the Latin *terra* – earth) in order to protect their rights and properties. They provide detailed descriptions of glebe lands, parsonages, out-buildings, local tithing customs and a variety of other matters. Their prime purpose was to identify the sources of incumbents' incomes; unusual sources were normally noted. Incumbents, churchwardens, other parish notables and neighbouring landowners are all likely to be named. Copies were frequently made for retention in the parish chest. In a few dioceses, registers of terriers were compiled. In others, they were bound together into books. Many have been published; some record society publications are listed below.

Visitations were recorded in act books, similar to those produced by ecclesiastical courts. These are likely to record action taken against the more serious offenders detected at the visitation. Frequently, such action constituted a reference to the ordinary ecclesiastical courts. The records of penances imposed, and of the certificates of performance sent in by those who carried them out, are discussed with the records of those courts (see below, pp.123–4).

Peculiars were not subject to bishops' visitations. They could, however, be visited by their superiors, such as deans and chapters. When this happened, the visitors produced documentation similar to that described above.

Further Reading
An introduction to glebe terriers is provided by:

• Barratt, D.M. 'Glebe terriers', in Munby, L.M., ed. *Short Guides to Records*. (Historical Association, 1972).

A number of county record society volumes have been devoted to glebe terriers. See, for example:

- Barratt, D.M., ed. *Ecclesiastical Terriers of Warwickshire Parishes*. (2 vols. Dugdale Society publications 22 & 27. 1955–71). Also includes replies to visitation queries for 1585.
- Hobbs, Steve, ed. *Wiltshire Glebe Terriers 1588-1827*. (Wiltshire Record Society 54. 2003).

Many bishops' queries and injunctions are printed in:

- Fincham, Kenneth, ed. *Visitation Articles and Injunctions of the Early Stuart Church*. (2 vols, Church of England Record Society 1 & 5. 1994–8).

Numerous visitation records, including returns to bishops' queries, churchwardens' presentments and various other documents, have been printed. Important publications include, amongst others:

Canterbury Diocese
- Gregory, Jeremy, ed. *The Speculum of Archbishop Thomas Secker*. (Church of England Record Society 2. 1996). Covers 1758–61.
- Sharp, W., and Whatmore, L.E., eds. *Archdeacon Harpsfield's Visitation, 1557*. (2 vols. Catholic Record Society, 45–46. 1950–1). For Canterbury; the last visitation in the reign of the Roman Catholic Queen Mary.

Chichester Diocese
- Ford, Wyn K., ed. *Chichester Diocesan Surveys, 1686 and 1724*. (Surrey Record Society 78. 1994).

Exeter Diocese
- Episcopal Visitation Returns, 1744 and 1779 [for Devon] **http://foda.org.uk/visitations/intro/introduction1.htm**

- Cook, Michael, ed. *The Diocese of Exeter in 1821: Bishop Carey's Replies to Queries before Visitation*. (2 vols. Devon & Cornwall Record Society 3–4. 1958–60).

Lichfield and Coventry Diocese
- Austin, M.R., ed. *The Church in Derbyshire in 1823-4: the parochial visitation of Rev. Samuel Butler, Archdeacon of Derby in the Diocese of Lichfield and Coventry*. (Derbyshire Archaeological Society Record Series 5. 1972).
- Beckett, John, Tranter, Margery, and Bateman, Wendy, eds. *Visitations from the Archdeaconry of Derby 1718-1824*. (Derbyshire Record Society 29. 2003). Actually replies to Bishops' queries.
- Robinson, D., ed. *Visitations of the Archdeaconry of Stafford, 1829-1841*. (Staffordshire Record Society 10. 1980).

Lincoln Diocese
- Brinkworth, E.R.C., ed. *Episcopal Visitation Book for the Archdeaconry of Buckingham, 1662*. (Buckinghamshire Record Society 7. 1947).
- Broad, John, ed. *Bishop Wake's Summary of Visitation returns from the Diocese of Lincoln 1706-1715*. (2 vols. Records of Social and Economic History new series 49–50. Oxford University Press for the British Academy, 2012). Volume 2 covers counties other than Lincolnshire.
- Cole, R.E.G., ed. *Speculum dioceseos Lincolniensis sub episcopis Gul Wake et Edm Gibson, A.D.1705-1723. Pt.1. Archdeaconries of Lincoln and Stow*. (Lincoln Record Society 4. 1913).

Llandaff Diocese
- Guy, John R., ed. *The Diocese of Llandaff in 1763: the Primary Visitation of Bishop Ewer*. (South Wales Record Society 7. 1991).

Norwich Diocese
- Williams, J.F., ed. *Diocese of Norwich: Bishop Redman's Visitation, 1597. Presentments in the Archdeaconries of Norwich, Norfolk, and Suffolk*. (Norfolk Record Society 18. 1946).

Oxford Diocese
- Peyton, Sidney A., ed. *The Churchwardens' Presentments in the Oxfordshire Peculiars of Dorchester, Thame and Banbury.* (Oxfordshire Record Society 10. 1928).

Salisbury Diocese
- *Churchwardens' Presentments 1662.* (4 vols. Wiltshire Family History Society, 2014).

Winchester Diocese
- Penfold, P.A., ed. *Call Book for the Episcopal Visitations of the Diocese of Winchester, 1581 and 1582: portions relating to the Archdeaconry of Surrey.* (Surrey Record Society 23. 1956).
- Ward, W.R., ed., *Parson and Parish in Eighteenth-Century Hampshire: Replies to Bishops' Visitations.* (Hampshire Record Series 13. 1995). Covers returns for 1725, 1765 and 1788.
- Ward, W.R., ed. *Parson and Parish in Eighteenth-Century Surrey: Replies to Bishops' Visitations.* (Surrey Record Society 34. 1994). Covers returns for 1725, 1764 and 1788.

Worcester Diocese
- Ransome, Mary, ed. *The State of the Bishopric of Worcester, 1782-1808.* (Worcestershire Historical Society new series 6. 1968).

York Diocese and Province
- Kitching, C.J., ed. *The Royal Visitation of 1559: Act Book for the Northern Province.* (Surtees Society 187. 1975).
- Hoskin, Philippa, ed. *A Decent, Regular and Orderly State? Parochial Visitations of the Archdeaconries of York and the East Riding.* (Borthwick Texts and Studies 40. Borthwick Institute, 2010). Covers 1720s and 1730s.
- Ollard, S.L., and Walker, P.C., eds. *Archbishop Herring's visitation returns, 1743.* (Yorkshire Archaeological Society Record Series 71, 72, 75, 77 & 79. 1928–30).

- Royle, Edward, ed. *Bishop Bickersteth's Visitation Returns for the Archdeaconry of Craven, 1858.* (Borthwick Texts and Studies 37. Borthwick Institute, 2009).
- Fisher, Howard, ed. *Church Life in Georgian Nottinghamshire: Archbishop Drummond's Parish Visitation Returns 1764.* (Thoroton Society Record Series 46. 2012). Replies to bishops' queries.

B. DIOCESAN COURTS

In 1070, William I decreed that the bishops were to hold separate courts to judge causes brought before them under ecclesiastical law.[8] His decree led to the gradual development of ecclesiastical courts, which was only interrupted by the Interregnum. Ecclesiastical courts were still flourishing in the eighteenth century. By then, prosecutions for failing to attend church had mostly ceased, but the courts were still heavily used to discipline those who offended against community morality, such as adulterers, brawlers and the parents of bastards. Two-thirds of the cases heard in the Norwich Consistory Court in the 1740s concerned fornication and adultery.[9] The courts also heard many disputes between neighbours. Like the secular Justices of the Peace, ecclesiastical judges frequently sought to reconcile those in dispute, rather than simply passing judgement on the matter in dispute.

The jurisdiction of church and secular courts frequently overlapped; many cases could have been heard by either Quarter Sessions[10] or by the Archdeaconry courts; indeed, occasionally some were heard by both. Litigants frequently preferred to use the ecclesiastical courts rather than Quarter Sessions. Most cases came before church courts as the result of lay initiative.

The role of the church courts was profoundly affected by what happened between 1641 and 1660, and they never recovered the full extent of their pre-war business.[11] Decline set in towards the end of the century, and continued throughout the eighteenth century. In 1830, the Royal Commission on Ecclesiastical Courts reported that there had only been fifty correctional cases in the whole country between 1827 and 1829.[12] In the ensuing decades, most of the

The Bishop of Norwich's Consistory Court sometimes sat at King's Lynn in Norfolk.

powers of the ecclesiastical courts were removed. Today, their role is confined to the exercise of faculty jurisdiction over church property, and to disciplining errant clergy.

Within the diocese, ecclesiastical courts operated at two levels. The Consistory Court covered the whole diocese, and was superior to the Archdeaconry courts, although in practice litigants could frequently choose the most convenient court. Bishops and archdeacons rarely sat in judgement themselves; rather, they appointed judges to hear cases on their behalf. The Archdeacon's judge was known as the Official. Sometimes bishops appointed Commissaries who also sat in Archdeaconry courts. The bishop's Consistory Court was presided over by his Vicar General in office causes, or the Official Principal in instance causes.[13] These two posts might be combined in the Chancellor of the Diocese. Another

The record of a faculty at Lymington in Hampshire.

important court official was the Registrar, frequently a layman, who kept the records we now use, and who was responsible for the issue of citations. His efficiency was crucial to the effectiveness of the courts he administered. Apparitors, sometimes known as Summoners or Mandataries, delivered citations, and called witnesses on court days. They were expected to detect any offences committed in their deaneries, investigate information that came from other sources, check whether churchwardens and clergy were performing their duties, and even to report to the bishop any deaths amongst the clergy.[14] The court was attended by a number of proctors, who acted as solicitors on behalf of their clients. Surrogates could also be appointed from amongst the diocesan clergy to act locally in taking oaths, signing affidavits, issuing licences, and similar activities.

In addition to the Consistory and Archidiaconal Courts, a few dioceses had other courts; for example, the Chancery Court was established in the Diocese of York in the fifteenth century. Peculiars had their own courts. The bishop himself sometimes also held an Audience court, in which he presided in person. Unfortunately, post-medieval records are scarce. Provincial courts will be discussed later, as will probate courts.

Much of the work of ecclesiastical judges was non-contentious, concerned with acts of validation, admission and authorization: proving wills, issuing licences admitting clergymen to benefices. These topics are all discussed below. Our immediate concern is with the more strictly judicial work of the courts.

The courts in the sixteenth century played an important role in enforcing the Reformation settlement.[15] The Royalist settlement of

The Consistory Court at Chester.

the church after the Restoration in 1660 was similarly enforced. And until the late eighteenth century both laity and clergy could be subject to intrusive court investigations of their morals. Judicial activity fell into two main categories, office and instance. Office business was promoted by court officials as a result of presentments by churchwardens or incumbents. It related primarily to disciplinary matters within the church, which could relate to both clergy and laity. They are sometimes referred to as 'correction' business, since it was the function of the bishop to correct his flock. The punishments the court imposed were intended to rescue the souls of offenders from sin, rather than to inflict retribution.

Failure to pay dues such as church rates, Easter offerings and especially tithes, formed an important part of court business. The morals of parishioners were considered to be within their purview, so matters such as marriage, fornication and adultery were dealt with – hence the cynic's view of them as the 'bawdy courts'. It might be added that prosecutions for fornication were frequently begun in order to protect the parish against having to pay for a bastard's upbringing, rather than out of any concern for the defendant's spiritual welfare. Sexual offences came to dominate office cases after 1689,[16] although they declined rapidly after an Act of 1787 required prosecution of fornication to take place within eight months of the offence being committed. Slander, brawling in church and unlawful intrusion into pews were amongst other moral issues dealt with. The courts sought to ensure that both clergy and laity stuck to the canons. Clergy who preached without a licence, or departed from the *Book of Common Prayer*, were prosecuted. So were churchwardens not properly sworn in, schoolmasters, surgeons and midwives who did not have licences (see below, pp.131–7), and executors who had not proved their wills. Those who refused to attend church, failed to receive the sacrament or attend catechism, and who would not bring their babies for baptism, were all liable to appear before an ecclesiastical judge.

Some offences that came before the church courts could also be prosecuted at Quarter Sessions, or dealt with by Justices of the Peace.

Quarter Sessions could impose severer penalties on recusants (those who refused to attend church), while Justices of the Peace could compel the fathers of bastards to pay maintenance for their children. In the seventeenth century, Justices were generally only likely to intervene if cases could not be satisfactorily settled by ecclesiastical court procedures. That was to change in the following century. As already noted, Justices of the Peace were increasingly more accessible and efficient than the sometimes remote ecclesiastical courts.

Office business also related to the administration of the church. Fabric was a matter of concern. Faculties approving alterations to the fabric of churches and church property were granted by judicial process. The person promoting alterations had to present a citation 'with intimation' against the rector and churchwardens, detailing the alterations proposed. This document had to be read publicly in church, in order to allow objections to be made. Many citations were concerned with seating, and give names of pewholders; others proposed the building of galleries or the entire replacement of churches. The courts were also concerned with dilapidations. If an incumbent neglected church property, allowing the chancel, the parsonage or other buildings to fall into disrepair, his living could be sequestered. And if he died or resigned, his estate could be sued by his successor to make up the damage caused.

Instance business was business brought before the court at the instance of a plaintiff, when he or she was in dispute with the defendant. It could also be initiated as a result of church-wardens' presentments, denunciations, informations, accusations and inquisitions. It was much more important to the court than office business.[17] In the mid-sixteenth century, disputes concerning matrimony, probate, tithes and defamation constituted nine-tenths of the instance cases which came before the courts of the Dioceses of Norwich and Winchester. Matrimonial causes prior to the nineteenth century were primarily concerned with the validity of marriages, rather than – as is the case today – the desire to separate. The law did not recognize divorce, although marriages could be annulled if they were not considered legally valid. Most matrimonial suits were brought by parties seeking to enforce the marriage contract. Tithe causes are discussed in Chapter 6; probate causes in Chapter 8.

Defamation causes constituted probably the most important single type of instance cause. People who were defamed wanted their libellers to suffer a short, sharp shock. That was frequently achieved merely by citing them to appear before the court. Most defamation causes were settled long before they reached sentence. Despite their prominence in the ecclesiastical courts, the number of cases gradually declined in the eighteenth century, especially after the Act of 1787 mentioned above required plaintiffs to commence a case within six months of the defamatory words being spoken. By the late 1820s, a mere 110 causes were being heard per annum in all ecclesiastical courts.[18]

A part of the reason for the decline, as has already been noted, was the more effective justice increasingly provided by Justices of the Peace. They could issue warrants for offenders to appear before them, and compel them to enter recognizances to either keep the peace or to appear at Quarter Sessions. Frequently they arbitrated between the parties. The notebook of Edmund Tew, the rector of Boldon (Co Durham),[19] and a Justice of the Peace, records numerous causes that he dealt with on his own initiative, without referring them to any court. Defamation was one of the major causes that came before him; so was bastardy. These cases could have been heard before ecclesiastical courts. But Tew was acting in his judicial capacity, not as a clergyman.

Whether cases were dealt with as office or instance causes depended on a variety of factors, such as the custom of the particular court, how the matter had come before the court, the pressure of business and the standing of the parties. Procedure in both office and instance business could be summary or plenary. Summary proceedings, allowing for the straightforward correction of faults, was mainly verbal, although both summary and plenary proceedings were recorded in act books. These were frequently written up in advance, with the decisions of the court written in later. They are particularly difficult to understand, due to bad handwriting, the inconsistent use of both Latin and English, the use of many abbreviations and the use of initials for both parties and the proctors. The cause papers (see below, pp.125–8), if they survive, are likely to be more informative.

Summary proceedings frequently arose from churchwardens' presentments at visitation, and were frequently dealt with then and there. Until the Civil War correction matters were recorded in the visitation books (sometimes known as *libri comperta*, or books of detection). Alternatively, the Registrar would cite the defendant to appear at the regular court. Citations stated the name of the defendant, the parish he lived in, and a brief summary of the case alleged against him. Citations were delivered by the apparitors, who had to make a sworn statement confirming delivery, made before a surrogate. They were returned to the court, where many were preserved. Service of a citation was frequently sufficient to bring about a settlement, and a third of causes in the sixteenth century went no further.[20]

If a case arose as a consequence of the defendant's reputation, or 'common fame', he could bring five or six neighbours with him as 'compurgators', to swear to his innocence. Compurgation was abolished in 1641. If the defendant failed in compurgation, and was found guilty, the sentence imposed had to be carried out by the offender's parish priest. He was issued with a schedule of penance or confession, which he was expected to certify and return to the court when sentence had been carried out. It is not surprising that, sometimes, the role of the individual clergyman in carrying out the orders of ecclesiastical courts was resented.

Only two sentences were possible for the laity: penance or excommunication. Alternatively, the offender might be merely admonished. The aim of the sentence was always pastoral; the sinner had to be rescued from sin and be set back upon the path of salvation. Penance depended on the sin. A slanderer might have to read a recantation in public, in front of the person they had offended. Fornicators had to stand in a white sheet, with a wand in their hand, without shoes, and read their confession in church – and perhaps in two or three different churches. In the sixteenth century, a beating might be administered by the parish priest. Alternatively, and especially when the defendant was of some status, the sentence might be commuted to a monetary payment, in which case the minister would be expected to receive the fine. He was supposed to use it for some charitable purpose, and had to certify that the fine had been paid by returning the schedule of penance to the court.

Excommunication[21] was a severer punishment. The lesser excommunication, involving deprivation of the right to attend church and receive the sacraments, was reserved for those who were contumacious, that is, they either refused to appear in court or they refused to accept their penance. Excommunication meant exclusion from church, and thus from the meeting place of the parish; excommunicates could not have a church wedding. The greater excommunication was for those who had committed much more serious sins, such as assault in church, clandestine marriage or persistent contumacy. They were supposed to be ostracized by fellow parishioners, and suffered various social and legal disabilities. They could not buy or sell anything, nor be employed; they could not sue in the courts, nor could they act as an executor or witness a will. They were excluded from parish office, and from the manorial homage (and thus could not hold land by copyhold). If they died, they could neither leave valid wills nor be buried in a consecrated place. Excommunication was supposed to make it impossible to trade or farm normally, or to fulfil social responsibilities.[22] Registrars frequently made lists of excommunicates, some of which survive.

The majority of excommunicates eventually sought absolution, which may be recorded in act books. Recusants, of course, did not accept the sentence. Bishop Bilson of Winchester wrote that excommunication was 'a penalty utterly despised by the recusant gentry'.[23] Many others also remained excommunicate. After they had remained excommunicate for more than forty days, a signification could be directed to the Court of Chancery, who would then issue a writ of *De excommunicato capiendo* to have them arrested and imprisoned. Such *significavits*[24] are now in the National Archives for the periods 1220–1611 (class C85) and 1727–1842 (class C207/1-12 & 23). For Cheshire, some *significavits*, 1378–1690 (with gaps) are in CHES 38/25/4-6. Significations were, however, relatively rare, even in the sixteenth century. Many of those who remained contumacious simply removed themselves to another jurisdiction. To the local community, their disappearance may have seemed a satisfactory outcome of legal proceedings. Significations were expensive for ecclesiastical court officials, and frequently pointless if offenders could not be found.[25] It was better to prosecute recusants in Quarter Sessions, where harsher penalties could be imposed.

Penance and excommunication could also be imposed on clergy, but a wider range of penalties was also available to the courts.[26] Clergy could be suspended from office, their income could be sequestered and they could be deprived. Deprivation was used on a number of occasions when governments changed religious policy. When Queen Mary reverted to Catholicism, clergy who had married under her predecessor were deprived. When Elizabeth succeeded, those who refused the Oath of Supremacy were likewise deprived. As has already been seen, many Royalist clergy were deprived during the Interregnum, and some 2,000 were ejected in 1662. Non-jurors who refused the oath of allegiance when William of Orange seized the throne in 1688 were deprived.

Deprivation was rarely used on other occasions. Suspension and sequestration were generally effective in securing the aims of the courts. Suspension was likely to bring contumacious clergymen to heel, and to encourage lesser offenders to improve their efficiency or their knowledge. Non-residence (including the failure to provide a curate) and dilapidations could provoke the sequestration of a clergyman's income, and compel the offender to take remedial action. In the sixteenth century the bishops had their own prisons, although most of their occupants (until 1576) were in fact laymen who had claimed the fictitious 'benefit of clergy' when accused of criminal behaviour before a lay judge.[27]

125

Plenary procedure was conducted by producing written documents in court. Most correction causes ended with the initial citation, so were not heard in plenary form. However, where plenary procedures were used, the resultant documentation provides valuable eyewitness evidence of the daily life and social mores of our ancestors. Act books record the dates assigned for each procedure, the names of proctors, and the fees due to the Registrar. Cases were frequently postponed, so it may be necessary to consult the record for several successive sessions in order to trace the progress of a case through the court. Postponement frequently led to no further action.

Judges (in office cases) or plaintiffs made a written statement of the case, known as the *libel*. The facts of the case would be 'propounded' in numbered format. A 'personal answer' was demanded from the defendant; if, as was usual, the case was denied, the answer would be a formal denial of each paragraph of the libel, delivered by the proctor of the accused. The libel was then referred to as an allegation. A *term probatory* would be assigned for the prosecution to produce witnesses, who would be summoned by citations known as 'compulsories'. Their depositions would be written down by the Registrar in private (to avoid collusion), before being produced in court. Surrogates were sometimes appointed in order to take depositions locally. Witnesses would be questioned by means of 'interrogatories' submitted by the proctors of the adverse side. Depositions answering interrogatories are sometimes written on the same sheet. Sometimes depositions led to further questioning by means of replications. Depositions are particularly valuable evidence; they provide us with sometimes detailed eyewitness accounts of the everyday lives of our ancestors. Exhibits such as testimonials from local clergy, excerpts from parish registers, title deeds, plans, or tithe agreements, might also be placed before the court, and may still survive amongst court records. The defendant could bring 'exceptions' before the court, raising technical points of law, at any point in the proceedings; such exceptions had to be considered immediately.

Agreement between the parties frequently halted cases before sentence could be passed. Sometimes, prohibitions emanating from the secular courts also halted proceedings. Financial matters were frequently regarded as being outside of the remit of the ecclesiastical courts. This particularly affected tithe causes (see above, pp.99–102). Probate causes where freehold property was involved might similarly be removed. Such causes gradually ceased to be heard in the ecclesiastical courts.

Once the evidence had been heard, sentence was pronounced. Confusingly, at least in Lichfield Diocese,[28] two versions of the sentence were produced, one by the plaintiff, one by the defendant. The one signed by the judge was legally binding, although they tell us little about the reasons for his judgement. That has to be inferred from the other trial papers; such inferences must frequently be very tentative. Once the sentence had been signed, bills of costs, with monitions to pay, were presented to the party who had to pay the bill. These bills can help us trace the progress of a case through the court. Fees dues from the poor were, however, frequently excused. A copy of the sentence was sent to the Archdeacon or Rural Dean to be published in the locality where the defendant resided. Parties were expected to abide by the decision of the court, or face excommunication.

The effectiveness of penance and excommunication as punishments depended on the cooperation of local people. The sixteenth-century Reformation seriously weakened respect for these spiritual censures, demoralized those who ran the courts, and imposed new burdens on administrators which threatened the delicate balance between official and popular demands. The ejections of 1662, and the growth of Nonconformity, led to even less respect for excommunication. Spiritual censures against Nonconformists became a complete irrelevance, and merely made the courts an object of derision. Even where there was support for punishment, as in the case of fornication (which was likely to cost ratepayers money), cases gradually ceased to come before the spiritual courts in the eighteenth and nineteenth centuries. Justices of the Peace and the secular courts were better able to provide remedies. Nevertheless, the ecclesiastical courts, at least in some places, remained vigorous throughout most of the eighteenth century. The number of sexual offences heard in North Lancashire did not peak until the 1770s, although admittedly decay had set in earlier in the industrial districts to the south. The administrative structures of the ecclesiastical courts remained resilient until almost the end of the century. In the nineteenth century, however, excommunication for contumacy ceased in 1813, tithe causes were removed from their jurisdiction in 1836, defamation causes in 1855, matrimonial causes in 1857 and probate causes in 1858.

Cause papers were preserved in a variety of different ways. In some courts, each type of document was filed separately in perhaps yearly bundles. Depositions were sometimes bound into books, and/or registered. In other courts, all of the papers in a particular cause were bundled together. There was, however, no consistency in filing arrangements, which varied not only between courts, but from year to year within the same court.

Using ecclesiastical court records is not easy. The documents are frequently not very well preserved; the heavy use of abbreviations, combined with poor handwriting, may pose difficulties. Surviving evidence for a particular case may be fragmentary: there may be presentments and citations without any other documentation, or depositions and replications without sentences. Despite these difficulties, the records do contain a great deal of valuable information, and persistence is likely to have its reward.

Further Reading

The history of the church courts is outlined by:

- Outhwaite, R.B. *The Rise and Fall of the English Ecclesiastical Courts, 1500-1860*. (Cambridge University Press, 2006).
- Houlbrooke, Ralph. *Church Courts and the People during the English Reformation, 1520-1570*. (Oxford University Press, 1979).
- Ingram, Martin. *Church Courts, Sex and Marriage in England, 1570-1640*. (Cambridge University Press, 1987).

For the Northern Province, see:

- Marchant, Ronald A. *The Church Under the Law: Justice, Administration and Discipline in the Diocese of York 1560–1640.* (Cambridge University Press, 1969). Includes brief biographical notes on advocates and others connected with the courts.

See also:

- Marchant, Ronald A. *The Puritans and the Church Courts in the Diocese of York, 1560-1642.* (Longmans, 1960). Includes lists of Puritan clergy.

The records of ecclesiastical courts are described by:

- Chapman, Colin. *Sin, Sex, and Probate: Ecclesiastical Courts, Officials, & Records.* (2nd ed. updated, Lochin Publishing, 2009). Originally published as *Ecclesiastical Courts: their Officials, & their Records.*
- Tarver, Anne. *Church Court Records: an Introduction for Family and Local Historians.* (Phillimore, 1995).

Many examples of records from the church courts are printed in:

- Hair, Paul, ed. *Before the Bawdy Court: Selections from Church Court and other Records relating to the correction of moral offences in England, Scotland, and New England. 1300-1800.* (Paul Elek Books, 1972).

For an index of cases heard in the Consistory Court of London, see:

- Webb, Cliff. *London's Bawdy Courts, vol.1. 1703-1713.* (Society of Genealogists, 1999).

Cause papers from the Diocese of York have been digitized at:

• Cause Papers in the Diocesan Courts of the Archbishopric of York, 1300–1858
  www.hrionline.ac.uk/causepapers

For guidance in the use of this database, together with a few examples of cases heard by the court, see:

• Borthwick Institute for Archives: What are Cause Papers?
  www.york.ac.uk/borthwick/holdings/guides/research-guides/what-are-causepapers
• Hoskin, Philippa, Sandall, Simon, and Watson, Emma. 'The Court Records of the Diocese of York 1300–1858: An Under-Used Resource', *Yorkshire Archaeological Journal* 83(1) (2011), pp.148–67.

Depositions from records of the Diocese of Oxford are printed in:

• Howard-Drake, Jack, ed. *Oxford Church Courts: depositions, 1542-1550.* (Oxfordshire Archives, 1992). A number of further volumes print depositions up to 1639. This project is further discussed in:
• Howard-Drake, Jack. 'Church court records and the local historian', *Local Historian* 25(1) (1995), p.7–16.

Faculty records are discussed and listed in:

• Evans, Peter. *Church Fabric in the York Diocese, 1613-1899: the records of the archbishops' faculty jurisdiction: a handlist.* (Borthwick Texts & Calendars 19. 1995).

For Archdeaconry records, much useful advice is provided by:

• Brinkworth, E.R. 'The Study and Use of Archdeacons' Court Records: illustrated from the Oxford Records (1566-1759)',

Transactions of the Royal Historical Society (4th series 25. 1943), pp.93–119.

See also:

- Webb, C.C., and Smith, David M. 'Archdeacons' Records' in Thompson, K.M., ed. *Short Guides to Records. Second series: Guides 25-48*. (Historical Association, 1997), pp.38–43.

For the records of the Archdeaconry of Nottingham, see:

- The University of Nottingham: Manuscripts and Special Collections: Archdeaconry of Nottingham **www.nottingham.ac.uk/manuscriptsandspecialcollections /collectionsindepth/archdeaconry/introduction.aspx**

Good examples of archdeaconry court records in print are provided by:

- Brinkworth, E.R., ed. *The Archdeacon's Court: liber actorum, 1584*. (2 vols. Oxfordshire Record Society, 23–24. 1942).
- Christie, Peter, ed. *Of Chirche-Reves and of Testaments: the Church, Sex, and Slander in Elizabethan North Devon*. (Devon Family History Society, 1994).
- Emmison, F.G. *Elizabethan Life: Morals & the Church Courts*. (Essex County Council, 1973). Essex examples.

For a published collection of defamation causes that came before both ecclesiastical and royal courts, see:

- Helmholz, R.H., ed. *Select Cases on Defamation to 1600*. (Selden Society 101. 1985).

C. BISHOPS' LICENCES
Schoolmasters, surgeons, physicians, and midwives all required licences from a bishop.[29] Their religious opinions, their morals and

their practical knowledge, were all subject to episcopal oversight. Parish clerks, curates and preachers also required licences (see below, p.179). Applications for licences, nominations, and testimonials frequently survive, as do records of the licences issued.[30] Failure to obtain a licence might lead to presentment by the churchwarden, and to proceedings in the ecclesiastical courts, as discussed above.

Licences granted in the Diocese of Canterbury are listed in:

• Willis, A.J. *Canterbury Licences (General), 1568-1646*. (Phillimore, 1972).

i. Surgeons and Physicians

A statute of 1511 required physicians and surgeons to be examined by four practitioners, and licensed by a bishop, before they could practice. Licensing was only necessary for those without degrees, although some who had degrees also sought licences. Many practised without licences, sometimes only applying for them when they needed the support of the law to compel their patients to pay their bills, or perhaps so that they could charge higher fees.

Applications and testimonials for licences survive amongst diocesan archives. Testimonials were frequently certificates of competence, signed by medical practitioners – although the requirement for four examiners was frequently ignored. Many testimonials bear only two signatures, and sometimes included clergymen rather than practitioners. Some were signed by patients. Others took the form of communal petitions, with numerous signatures, rather than certificates of competence. Some applicants were actually examined by practitioners. That might be necessary for applicants who knew no-one willing to support them. Noah Mahun of St Endellion (Cornwall) had to visit Exeter for examination. His testimonial reads: 'Wee Chyrurgeons of the Citty of Exon doe hereby certifie to your Lord shipp that wee have strictly examined Mr Noah Mahun of St Endellion . . . in the art of chirurgery, who wee finde fitt and qualified therein, and who deserves your Lordshipps lycence for the performing thereof . . . 1 August 1709. [signed:] [Thomas] Downton surgeon. John Pearce surgeon'.[31]

Grants of licences were recorded in act books. They were made to practice in specific geographical areas, e.g. in a particular town or county, throughout a diocese, or indeed (by the Archbishop) throughout the Province. Some licences were granted during visitations, so information may occasionally be found in visitation records. Information can also sometimes be found in the answers to bishops queries discussed above. Not everyone who applied for a licence was granted one; in the early eighteenth century, perhaps 40 per cent of applicants in the Diocese of Exeter were turned down.

Ecclesiastical supervision of medics flourished for over two centuries, but declined as the eighteenth century progressed. Over 35,000 medics, identified partly from these licences, are listed in:

• Wallis, J., and Wallis, R.V. *Eighteenth Century Medics (subscriptions, licences, apprenticeships).* (2nd ed. Newcastle upon Tyne: Project for Historical Bibliography, 1988).

Licencees in the Diocese of London are listed in:

• Bloom, J. Harvey, and James, R. Rutson. *Medical Practitioners in the Diocese of London under the act of 3 Henry VIII, c.II: an annotated list 1529-1725.* (Cambridge University Press, 1935).

For the rest of the country, a list for the early seventeenth century is available:

• Raach, John. *A Directory of English Country Physicians, 1603-1643.* (Dawsons of Pall Mall, 1962).

The Archbishop of Canterbury could grant licences throughout the Southern Province, as well as in his own diocese. His Provincial licensing authority was exercised through his Vicar General, and also through the Faculty Office; the latter could grant licences to practice in the Northern Province as well. The Archbishop's licencing records, except those for his own Diocese, are now held by Lambeth Palace Library, and are indexed at:

• Lambeth Palace Library Research Guide: Medical Licences Issued by the Archbishop of Canterbury 1535–1775
  www.lambethpalacelibrary.org/files/Medical_Licences.pdf

For licensing procedure, and for its importance, see:

• Guy, John R. 'The episcopal licensing of physicians, surgeons and midwives', *Bulletin of the History of Medicine* 56 (1982), pp.528–42.
• Harley, David. 'Bred up in the Study of that Faculty: Licensed Physicians in North-West England 1660-1760', *Medical History* 38 (1994), pp.398–420.
• Mortimer, Ian. 'Diocesan Licensing and Medical Practitioners in South-West England, 1660–1780', *Medical History* 48(1) (2004), pp.49–68.

ii. Midwives

Midwives had to be licensed in the same way as surgeons, and similar records survive, although we do not know when licensing commenced.[32] A midwife's oath from the mid-sixteenth century included various promises to maintain the highest standards of medical care. She was required to avoid being a party to Roman Catholic baptisms, and to report to the authorities any child not baptised according to Anglican rites. She was expected to extract information about the fathers of illegitimate babies from their (sometimes) unwilling mothers. Midwives' inquiries (perhaps made during labour) may be recorded in bastardy examinations, or sometimes in court proceedings. A testimonial sent into court by one Norfolk midwife recorded that 'we examined hyr in moste labor and trauaylle who was the chylldes father and she sayd that no nother man was the father but Thomas Ryder'.[33]

The Church also sought to ensure that midwives properly baptised weak or sickly babies who were not expected to survive. The Archbishop of York required his clergy to 'openly in the church teach and instruct the mydwiefes of the very words and form of baptisme to thentents that they may use them perfectly well and none oder'. Babies baptised by midwives were frequently re-baptised in church, and parish registers may record the fact. Midwives took their ecclesiastical duties seriously: in 1690, the rector of Chelsea reported that Elizabeth Forrest, who was applying for a licence, 'doth constantly bring her women whom she delivers to the church to pay their thanks in publick and their children to receive publick baptism'.

In the seventeenth-century Diocese of London, the grant of a licence required six women to testify under oath to their personal knowledge of the applicant's expertise. They, together with the applicant, were expected to appear in person before the bishop, as well as providing testimonial certificates. The licence fee was high, perhaps £1 or £2, helping to ensure that only dependable and economically viable women were licensed. Once the licence had been issued, it had to be produced regularly at ecclesiastical visitations, and its production may be noted in visitation records.

For Yorkshire, midwives nominations (i.e. testimonials) have been indexed in:

• Grundy, Joan E. *History's Midwives, including a c17th and c18th Yorkshire Midwives Nominations Index*. (Federation of Family History Societies, 2003).

A detailed study of London midwives is provided by:

• Evenden, Doreen. *The Midwives of Seventeenth-Century London*. (Cambridge University Press, 2000).

iii. Schoolmasters' Licences

Schoolmasters exercised a considerable degree of influence over their pupils. The authorities were concerned to ensure that the religious teaching they provided conformed with the established religion. Royal injunctions of 1559, confirmed by canons in 1571, required them to obtain licences from their bishop.[34] Masters had to submit nominations and testimonials when applying for a licence. These might be provided by a private patron, a minister or the governors of a school. The testimonial normally stated (at least in the Northern Province) that the nominee was of good moral character, a regular communicant, a supporter of the royal supremacy and that he had adequate academic qualifications. It might be annotated with a note of the date on which the licence was granted. The grant of schoolmasters' licences may be recorded in a register. All of these documents may indicate the educational qualifications of licence applicants.

At various times, schoolmasters also had to subscribe to various articles, and to take various oaths. From 1563, they were required to subscribe to the supremacy of the Crown. Canon 77 of 1603 required subscription to the first and third articles of the Thirty-Nine Articles. The post-Restoration Act of Uniformity of 1662 required school-masters to declare that 'it is not lawful . . . to take arms against the King . . . and that I will conform to the liturgy of the Church of England as it is now by law established'; they were also required to declare that the Solemn League and Covenant (which had been taken by many Parliamentary supporters) was 'an unlawful Oath, and imposed upon the subjects of this realm against the known laws and liberties of this Kingdom'. Subscription books in Diocesan archives are likely to date from 1662, if not earlier.

Some other oaths were taken in secular courts, but it is appropriate to mention them here. Between 1689 and 1702, schoolteachers had to take the oaths of allegiance and supremacy, and the oath against the doctrine of transubstantiation (the belief that bread and wine became the Lord's flesh and blood when consecrated). These oaths were taken either in the Courts of King's Bench and Chancery, or at Quarter Sessions. An Act of 1714 required schoolmasters to take an oath declaring their allegiance to the House of Hanover. The rolls recording these oaths are now either in the

National Archives (class C 214), or in County Record Offices. The requirement for licensing withered away in the late eighteenth and early nineteenth centuries; it finally ceased in 1869.

For a general discussion of schoolmasters' licensing, see:

• Tate, W.E. 'The Episcopal licensing of Schoolmasters in England', *Church Quarterly Review* 157 (1956), pp.426–32.

D. DIOCESAN PUBLICATIONS

The diocesan calendar was a product of nineteenth-century reform.[35] These annual publications were intended to nurture diocesan consciousness. The earliest was produced for the Diocese of Lichfield in 1856; others rapidly followed. They followed a standard pattern, disseminating diocesan information of varied kinds. There would probably be a brief biography of the bishop, and potted histories of the diocese and the cathedral. Details of provincial and diocesan officers, and of cathedral staff, would be given. Statistical information on parishes included such information as their population, church accommodation, and school provision, perhaps with the names of incumbents. The various Anglican charities operating in the diocese were listed. There might be architectural notes on new (and sometimes old) buildings. Recent ordinations would be listed, so would recent clergy deaths.

These calendars are still published in some dioceses, although their content has been adapted to current needs. They provide an invaluable base from which to research local church history, and enable the identification of clergy, diocesan officers and the local officers of charities.

E. THE RECORDS OF LOYALTY

The importance of oaths of loyalty in early modern England was considerable. They compelled subjects to be obedient to their rulers, under the threat of eternal damnation if they failed to do so. Reference has already been made to the various oaths that had to be taken by certain professions. For clergy oaths, see p.183. A number of other loyalty oaths were taken more widely, for example, the Protestation Oath of 1641/2,[36] the Solemn League and Covenant of 1643, the Association Oath of 1696 and the 1723 Oath of Allegiance. These are outside of the scope of this book, as they are not ecclesiastical records, nor do they specifically identify Anglicans.

The cooperation of the Church was, however, required in administering the check on loyalty imposed by the Test Act of 1673. It required both civil and military office-holders to prove their loyalty by receiving holy communion from a Church of England clergyman, thus demonstrating that they were loyal Anglicans. The clergyman concerned issued them with a sacrament certificate, confirming they had taken Holy Communion according to Anglican rites. Between 1689 and 1702 these documents were also required from beneficed clergy, university members, lawyers, schoolteachers and preachers.

It is important to appreciate that a sacrament certificate does not necessarily mean that its subject was a loyal churchman. Many Nonconformists had been reluctant to separate from the Church of England, and were prepared to attend an occasional service and take communion. The need to obtain a sacrament certificate in order to hold a public office meant that many Nonconformists practised occasional conformity. It can be difficult to distinguish in Anglican records between Nonconformity and slack religious observance.

Sacrament certificates may be found amongst Quarter Sessions records, and in The National Archives, series C 224, KB 22, E 196, and CHES 4. Most of The National Archives' certificates (except those in CHES 4 for Cheshire) relate to the London region. Certificates give names of communicants, places, and signatures of ministers, churchwardens, and witnesses. They ceased in 1828.

F. PROVINCIAL COURTS

The Archbishop of Canterbury was both a diocesan bishop, and head of his province. He operated provincial courts in addition to his diocesan courts. The Court of Arches exercised his appellate jurisdiction. The Audience Court originated as the personal court of the Archbishop, although in practice it became the court of the Vicar General. The Court of Faculties (the Faculty Office) dealt with administrative matters which had formerly been under Papal jurisdiction. The Prerogative Court was responsible for probate, and will be discussed in Chapter 8. All of these courts followed procedures, and produced documents, similar to those in Diocesan courts.

The Court of Arches, which takes its names from the arches in the church of St Mary le Bow (where it once sat), heard appeals against decisions of Consistory Courts, and of the Prerogative Court. Probate occupied much of its attention, but it also heard cases concerned with marriage, tithe, defamation, morals and a variety of other ecclesiastical matters. Its records are held by Lambeth Palace Library and have been microfilmed:

- *Records of the Court of Arches 1554-1911: Lambeth Palace Library.* 105 microfilm reels. (Chadwyck-Healey, c.1983).

There is a published index to these records:

- Houston, J. *Index of Cases in the Records of the Court of Arches at Lambeth Palace Library 1660-1912.* (Index Library 85. British Record Society, 1972).

The Audience Court, supposedly set up for the Archbishop to hear cases personally, in practice became the court of his Vicar General. It dealt with administrative matters and appeals, exercising a concurrent jurisdiction with the Court of Arches. The act books of the Vicar General, which include information relating both to the Province, and to the Diocese of Canterbury, are indexed in:

- Dunkin, Edwin Hadlow Wise, et al, eds. *Index to the Act Books of the Archbishops of Canterbury, 1663-1859.* (Index Library 55 & 63. British Record Society, 1929–38).

The Faculty Office, based in London, was an administrative

department established after the Reformation concerned with the issue of faculties, licences and dispensations formerly issued in the name of the Pope. Its earliest registers include clergy licences and dispensations dealing with matters such as pluralities and non-residence, as well as marriage licences:

• Chambers, D.S., ed. *Faculty Office Registers 1534-1549: a calendar of the first two registers of the Archbishops of Canterbury's Faculty Office*. (Clarendon Press, 1966).

For later marriage licences issued by the Vicar General, and by the Faculty Office, see above, pp.82–4.

The Northern Province had a similar range of courts, although there was no clear differentiation between Provincial courts and those of the Diocese of York. The Archbishop's Chancellor presided over both the Court of Audience or Chancery Court (as Vicar General), and the York Consistory Court (as Official Principal). There was a separate Court of Exchequer, and a Prerogative Court, both exercising probate jurisdiction. Reference has already been made to the York Diocesan cause papers.

For eighty years between c.1560 and c.1640, the supreme ecclesiastical court in England was the High Commission.[37] Under the Act of Supremacy of 1558, it had powers to fine and imprison that were not enjoyed by other ecclesiastical courts, and was given the role of enforcing ecclesiastical discipline throughout the country. It instigated disciplinary procedures against those whose social position might render them immune to prosecution in other courts. It was particularly concerned with recusancy, but also dealt with the whole range of topics covered by other ecclesiastical courts. Archbishop Laud used it against puritanism; consequently, it was abolished by the Long Parliament.

In practice, separate commissions operated in the two Provinces. Few records of the southern commission have survived,[38] but many act books, and court papers from the Northern Province are deposited at the Borthwick Institute **https://borthcat.york.ac.uk/index.php/archiepiscopal-courts**. For High Commission act books from the Diocese of Durham, see:

- Longstaffe, W. Hylton Dyer, ed. *The Acts of the High Commission Court within the Diocese of Durham*. (Surtees Society, 34. 1858).

In contrast to the High Commission, the High Court of Delegates merely continued to exercise the jurisdiction which had been exercised in the name of the Pope prior to the Reformation. It served as the final ecclesiastical appeal court from 1533 until 1833. Many causes relate to testamentary and matrimonial matters. Its records, including act books, cause papers, depositions, and other papers, are in the National Archives, class DEL. For details of the records of this court, see:

- Duncan, G.I.O. *The High Court of Delegates*. (Cambridge University Press, 1971).

G. CHAPTER RECORDS

At least since the Norman Conquest, there have been a number of great churches served by canons. The majority are cathedrals, that is, the seats of bishops. A few others, such as Ripon, Southwell, and Beverley, are (or were) minsters of Anglo-Saxon foundation. There are also a number of royal peculiars, such as Westminster Abbey and St. George's Chapel, Windsor. All of these foundations are governed by statutes, the more recent of which were granted by letters patent.[39] Many of these statutes have been printed by record societies and others.

These capitular bodies were governed by their chapters, consisting of deans and canons. The decisions of chapters are recorded in chapter act books. These are likely to record the installation of deans and canons, leases of capitular properties, appointments of treasurers, almsmen and all the capitular staff in between, orders concerning services, and much other minutiae of capitular administration.

A number of chapter act books, have been published. See, for example:

- Bailey, Derrick Sherwin, ed. *Wells Cathedral Chapter Act Book, 1666-83.* (Somerset Record Society 72. 1973).
- Eward, Suzanne, ed. *Gloucester Cathedral Chapter Act Book 1616-1687.* (Gloucestershire Record Series 21. Bristol and Gloucestershire Archaeological Society, 2007). Includes biographical notes on Cathedral dignitaries.

From the sixteenth century onwards, it became usual for documents which received the chapter seal to be copied into a separate register, variously known as leiger books, lease books or patent books. These were likely to include deeds, leases, presentations to chapter livings, patents of chapter officers, and various other documents. Sometimes separate registers were kept for different types of documents. Deeds, surveys, rentals, accounts and other records relating to capitular estates were also likely to be preserved. Information concerning tenants of capitular properties is likely to be found in these records, perhaps including details of the lives named in their leases. Accounts are also likely to record the expenditure of chapters on cathedral fabric, the wages of servants, and other matters; these accounts are likely to mention many names.

Chapters (or sometimes individual prebendaries) frequently had jurisdictional rights over parishes, hundreds, manors and other governmental bodies, and maintained a variety of court records. In particular, many exercised peculiar jurisdiction over probate matters, and many wills can be found amongst capitular archives. They also sometimes conducted visitations in their peculiars. Sometimes chapters or their prebendaries granted marriage licences and even, like the bishops, collected transcripts of parish registers. Such records are similar (if not identical) in form to diocesan records described elsewhere in this book.

H. CHURCH COMMISSIONERS

The Ecclesiastical Commissioners were established in 1833, and made permanent in 1836. In 1946, they merged with Queen Anne's Bounty (see below, p.185) to become the Church Commissioners. The Commissioners are responsible for the administration of all church property, which was previously in the hands of bishops, deans and chapters, and other ecclesiastical bodies. As estates came into its hands, it had them surveyed and mapped; the resultant documentation is now held by the Church of England Record Centre, together with files relating to leasing, purchases, sales, drainage and capital investment. The Centre is administered by Lambeth Palace Library, whose leaflet on 'sources for church property' also describes a variety of other ecclesiastical property records:

• Lambeth Palace Library Research Guide: Sources for Church Property
  www.lambethpalacelibrary.org/files/Church_Property_0.pdf

I. THE CHURCH BUILDING COMMISSION 1818–1856

In 1818, and again in 1824, as was seen in Chapter 1, Parliament made substantial grants for the building of new churches. The Church Building Commission was established in order to administer these grants. Six hundred churches were built by the Commission before it was amalgamated with the Ecclesiastical Commission in 1856. They were often referred to as the Waterloo or Million Act churches. The Commission also had the power to sub-divide parishes, and to provide endowments.

The records of the Commission are held by the Church of England Record Centre. They are listed, together with the names of Commissioners, architects, and contractors, in:

• Port, M.H. *600 New Churches: the Church Building Commission 1818-1856*. (Spire Books, 2006).

Chapter 8

PROBATE RECORDS

A. PROBATE JURISDICTION

The ecclesiastical courts of the Church of England were responsible for the administration of probate in England and Wales. Executors proved their wills before them; administrators of intestate estates applied to them for letters of administration authorizing them to distribute the estate. It was not until 1858 that probate became a civil matter.

The origins of ecclesiastical probate jurisdiction lay in the fact that the Church had itself introduced the practice of writing wills, since testators were expected to leave pious legacies of land, which would be best secured by possession of a written proof of the bequest. By the sixteenth century, probate business occupied much of the time of Archdeaconry, Consistory and Prerogative Courts. Many peculiar courts also had probate jurisdiction.

B. TESTATORS

Not everyone made a will. If you were a pauper, or had no goods to bequeath, you did not need to make a will. If you were a widower with only one son, he would automatically inherit, and a will would not be necessary. If you were happy with the way in which your property would be distributed if you died intestate, there was no point in making a will. In the Northern Province, until 1692, the law only allowed one-third of personal property to be bequeathed. A third automatically went to the widow, the other third was divided between the children. Far fewer wills were made there than in the Southern Province, where the testator could bequeath the whole of his personal estate.

More than half the population were incapable of making valid wills before the nineteenth century. Married women had no property in their own right, so could only make a will with the permission of their husbands. Boys under the age of fourteen, and girls under the age of twelve, could not make them. Lunatics, excommunicates, felons and others were all excluded from will-making. Most wills made the point that the testator was 'of sound and perfect memory'; if you were not, your will would be invalid.

The majority of testators were men. Most were married men, or perhaps widowers. A few were widows; a few were unmarried, perhaps dying young.

C. THE PURPOSE OF WILLS

Between the sixteenth and the nineteenth centuries, the wills of married men were frequently written in order to protect the interests of widows and younger children. They usually include mention of all living children, although children who were still dependent were likely to receive the bulk of bequests. The latter had not already been provided for.

Wills should be seen as a stage in the process of inheritance. That process began when the oldest child was settled on his own farm or apprenticed to a trade; it ended when the widow died, or when orphaned minors came of age. It was regarded as the duty of the father to ensure his children's economic future, as far as he could. That duty was frequently carried out before death. Sons would be settled on their own farm, or apprenticed to some trade. Daughters would be found dowries and married off. The concern at death was to provide for those children who had not already been provided for, or to provide for the widow.

Widows were similarly concerned to ensure their dependent children's future. The wills of the childless generally include a wider range of legatees: brothers, sisters, servants, friends.

Some wills are foundation documents for substantial charities, and have been preserved by the trustees for that reason. Parish records frequently include the wills of the founders of parish charities. So do the archives of independent charities.

D. THE PROCESS OF WILL MAKING

Until the nineteenth century, the majority of wills were written just before death. Clergy were expected to encourage their parishioners to write wills whilst they were fit and healthy, but many thought that was tempting fate, and few did so. Many wills describe the testator as 'weak in body'. If he were not, he would probably not have had the will written.

There were exceptions, of course. Someone embarking on a long journey, or about to take part in some hazardous enterprise, might make a will first. If a will is dated well before death, the testator usually had a reason.

The process of will making began when the testator summoned his friends to witness his will, and summoned a scribe to write it. Occasionally, the testator might write it himself; such wills are known as 'holographs'. The scribe might be a friend or relative, but frequently either the clergy or a village attorney were summoned. The testator would instruct the scribe what to write; the scribe would then go away and prepare a draft for the testator to sign. Sometimes, the testator died having delivered his will orally, but before there was time for it to be written down. Such nuncupative wills were accepted by the probate courts until 1837, providing that they could be proved by witnesses.

E. THE CONTENT OF WILLS

Wills are one of the few documents in which our ancestors could directly express their opinions and character. They can therefore sometimes be intensely personal, and tell us much about family relationships. On the other hand, they were frequently written by a scribe according to a formula, and may not always be what they seem – although testators would have read them before they signed, unless they were illiterate.

Wills from the eighteenth century and earlier usually commence with a religious preamble, affirming the testator's faith. That preamble is frequently suspect; it may reflect the scribe's opinion, rather than that of the testator, or it may simply be reproduced from a handbook for writing wills. The less formulaic it is, the more likely it is to reflect the testator's own faith.

The principal content of wills are the bequests. Most of these are to family members, and it is an unusual will which does not make at least a token mention of all the testator's surviving children. Sometimes they might also mention children's spouses and even grandchildren. Small bequests are also frequently made to the church, the poor, and charity. These are likely to follow the religious preamble, and reflect the ecclesiastical origins of wills. Sometimes bequests were made to the church or a charity in the testator's birthplace, thus suggesting to us where further research might prove fruitful.

Testators were limited in the goods that they could bequeath. Probate courts only had jurisdiction over personal property, not real property. Thus freehold land could not be bequeathed. It generally descended automatically to the eldest son, by the rules of primogeniture. It did not pass through the process of probate, and is not usually recorded in inventories or accounts.

There are other reasons why probate records may not reveal the total wealth of a testator. The stage the testator had reached in the life cycle may also have had an impact. Some would have retired and handed much of their property over to their children before making their will. Debts owed by the deceased were not recorded, except in accounts. Seasonality may have had an impact on the value of agricultural produce and livestock recorded in inventories. Goods may have been removed by beneficiaries before an inventory was taken. It is essential to appreciate that the total wealth of testators may not be revealed by probate records.

After the bequests, the executor or executrix is frequently named. He or she is frequently also the residuary legatee, that is, the person who will receive the remainder of the estate after the legacies have been distributed. Executors were frequently drawn from those who stood to receive the greatest benefit from the will, that is, widows and younger children.

The final element of a will are the witnesses. At least two are usually named. They could be relatives, neighbours, fellow tradesmen, sometimes the scribe.

F. DOCUMENTING THE PROCESS OF PROBATE

Once death had taken place, the executor named in the will, or if there was no will the next of kin, had to obtain either a grant of probate or letters of administration from the appropriate probate court. If they failed to do so, churchwardens might present them at visitation, or apparitors might cite them to appear before the court. They would be required to enter an administration bond in order to obtain a grant. The bond might require them to produce an inventory, if they had not brought one with them, and to be prepared to compile an account showing how the estate had been distributed. Grants were recorded in act books.

Wills themselves were sometimes copied into will registers; original wills might be separately filed, or perhaps returned to the executor. Probate inventories were frequently attached to wills, although in some diocesan registries they were separately filed. Inventories provide descriptions of the material possessions of our ancestors. Sometimes they are very detailed. Conversely, the information provided can be very sparse. The amount of detail provided depended on the caprice of the appraisers, who might be neighbours, friends or fellow tradesmen. There were usually two appraisers, sometimes more. Their names should always be noted to see if their connection with the testator can be identified.

Inventories only include personal property, not freehold property (although leasehold property is included).[1] They enable us to picture the environment in which our ancestors lived: the rooms in their house, their beds, chairs and table boards, their fireside and kitchen implements, their clothing, their livestock in the yard and the tools of their trade. Their listings of household goods demonstrate how empty the houses of our sixteenth century ancestors were. Houses were for working in, sleeping in and eating in; they were emphatically not designed for relaxing in. By the eighteenth century, however, they were filling up – to such an extent that compiling inventories had become a much greater chore. Furthermore, from the point of view of the diocesan registrar, their numbers and bulk rendered storing them in diocesan repositories very difficult. By c.1750 inventories ceased to be compiled as a matter of routine.

Probate accounts are much scarcer than inventories. They were probably only compiled when there was a likelihood of dispute, or when the probate court thought it necessary to call for them. Wills record how testators wished their property to be distributed. Accounts show how it was actually distributed. They give the names of the deceased and the accountant. The charge or 'onus' gives the value of the inventory, with any adjustments made for incorrect valuation. The discharge shows how the deceased's goods were distributed. Funeral and probate expenses had to be met. The debts of the deceased (including the cost of care during his final illness) had to be paid. The expenses of an estate did not necessarily cease with the death of its owner. Cattle had to be cared for, crops had to be harvested, taxes had to be paid. The executor may have been asked to act as guardian for the deceased's children, in which case their food, clothing, and education had to be paid for. All of these costs were recorded in probate accounts, together with the amounts paid to legatees. If there was no will, the estate had to be divided according to law. After 1670, one-third went to the widow; the balance was equally divided amongst the children.

From c.1600, administrators, and sometimes executors too, were required to enter into administration bonds before being granted probate. These bound them to produce inventories and accounts, and to administer estates faithfully. They had a standard wording, set by an Act of 1670. Until 1733, the bond itself was written in Latin, and the condition of the obligation in English. Many are written on printed forms. Bonds identify administrators and executors, together with their sureties, giving their parishes and occupations. It may be worth trying to trace the relationships between sureties and administrators.

Oaths of executors and administrators were sometimes taken by local clergymen, who recorded them by annotating and returning their commissions. Renunciations of executorship can occasionally be found. Churchwardens' presentments (see pp.91–5) and apparitors' citations (see p.123) might identify executors who failed to prove testators' wills.

Disputes over wills were generally dealt with in the ecclesiastical courts, unless they concerned real estate, in which case they were heard in the Westminster secular courts. Probate cases generally concerned either the validity of wills and rival claims to administer estates, or the way in which executors or administrators actually carried out their duties. The procedures followed in the ecclesiastical courts, and the allegations, interrogatories, depositions, and other documents created, were described in Chapter 7.

G. FINDING PROBATE RECORDS

In order to trace probate records, it is necessary to identify the ecclesiastical courts which exercised jurisdiction. Technically, most wills should have been proved in the Archdeaconry court where the testator lived. If the testator had goods in more than one archdeaconry, then the diocesan Consistory Court had jurisdiction. If goods were in more than one diocese, then the Prerogative Court of either Canterbury or York had jurisdiction. In practice, prestige demanded that those who aspired to higher status should have their wills proved either in the Consistory Court, or in the Prerogative Court. There was, however, no hard and fast rule (except during the Interregnum, 1649–60, when there was only one probate court).[2] Prerogative court wills include many wills of labourers; conversely, some gentlemen had their wills proved in Archdeaconry Courts. In the early nineteenth century; wills were increasingly being proved in the Prerogative Courts, and provincial courts were losing their probate business; in the late 1820s, over 60 per cent of probate grants were made there.[3]

Many peculiar courts also had probate jurisdiction. For example, the majority of Uffculme (Devon) wills were proved in the court of a Prebend of Salisbury, and are now held by Wiltshire and Swindon History Centre.[4]

Most Archdeaconry and Consistory Court wills are held by local record offices. Many indexes to them have been published in the British Record Society's Index Library. These are listed at:

• British Record Society: Publications
  www.britishrecordsociety.org/publications

Index Library volumes have been digitized, and are now available (together with a few other indexes) at:

• Find My Past: England & Wales Published Wills & Probate Indexes, 1300–1858
  http://search.findmypast.co.uk/search-world-Records/england-and-wales-published-wills-and-probate-indexes-1300-1858

Millions of wills have been digitized, and are available on the internet. For example, The National Archives have digitized some (not all) of their extensive collection of wills from the Prerogative Court of Canterbury (class PROB 11). These are available via their Discovery catalogue **http://discovery.nationalarchives.gov.uk**. Most Welsh wills (other than those proved in the Prerogative Court) have been digitized by the National Library of Wales **www.llgc.org.uk/discover/nlw-resources/wills**. For the location of other probate records, see the Gibson guide noted below.

Further Reading
A detailed and up-to-date general guide to probate records is provided by:

• Raymond, Stuart A. *The Wills of Our Ancestors: a Guide to Probate Records for Family and Local Historians*. (Pen & Sword, 2014).

The records of the Prerogative Court of Canterbury are emphasized in:

- Grannum, Karen, and Taylor, Nigel. *Wills & Probate Records: a Guide for Family Historians*. (2nd ed. National Archives, 2009).

A detailed guide to the locations of probate records, which identifies digitized collections of wills, and provides a comprehensive list of indexes, is provided by:

- Gibson, Jeremy. *Probate Jurisdictions: Where to Look for Wills*, revised by Stuart A. Raymond. (6th ed. Family History Partnership, 2016).

Interesting essays on various aspects of researching probate records are included in:

- Arkell, Tom, Evans, Nesta, and Goose, Nigel, eds. *When Death do Us Part: understanding and interpreting the probate records of early modern England*. (Leopards Head Press, 2004).
- Riden, Philip, ed. *Probate Records and the Local Community*. (Alan Sutton, 1985).

Chapter 9

ANGLICAN CHARITIES, MISSIONS AND RELIGIOUS ORDERS: THEIR STAFF AND THEIR BENEFICIARIES

Churchmen were involved in a wide range of local and national charities and societies. These were usually established as responses to the needs of society. Education, the relief of poverty, the elimination of drunkenness, the provision of medical support and the promotion of thrift were all prominent aims of Anglican charities. Support for the church and its clergy were also important: some aimed to provide new churches, others to increase the numbers of clergy, yet others to support clergy and their families who had fallen on hard times. After the Reformation, lectureships and the provision of sermons attracted monetary support from the devout. In the nineteenth and twentieth centuries, that support went to missionary societies. The church was involved in many activities other than worship. Jeff Cox has described the extent of its involvement in a particular area as follows:

> In 1899 and 1900 churches and chapels in Lambeth alone sponsored at least 58 thrift, slate and friendly societies, 57 mothers' meetings, 36 temperance societies for children, 36 literary or debating societies for young men, 27 bible classes, 27 girls' or young women's club, 25 cricket, tennis, or other sports clubs, 25 savings or penny banks, 24 Christian Endeavour societies, 21 boot, coal, blanket, or clothing clubs,

19 temperance societies, 17 branches of the Boys Brigade or Church Lads' Brigade, 13 vocational or adult classes, 13 men's club, 10 gymnasiums (usually devoted to recreational classes of some sort), and 10 maternity societies'.[1]

Churches which provided such activities flourished. Those which failed to do so tended to be unsuccessful.

The records of charities can provide you with a great deal of information concerning both their supporters and their beneficiaries. Their activities were frequently of great importance in the day-to-day life of local churches, and of the societies in which they operated. Local involvement in charitable activities is frequently reflected in the records of parochial administration. Parochial support for a particular charity frequently indicates the parish priest's religious affiliations and beliefs.

It is not possible here to do more than provide a brief overview of charitable organizations. Discussion is mostly limited to specifically Anglican charities, although it is important to note that both clergy and laity were heavily involved in a range of other organizations, including many that were specifically ecumenical. The Charity Organization Society, for example, attempted to work closely with the Church of England, both locally and nationally, although its opposition to indiscriminate charity did not always go down well with district visitors from the churches.[2] The Boy Scouts **www.scoutsrecords.org** and Girl Guides based their troops in churches of all denominations, including the Church of England. Institutions as diverse as London's Foundling Hospital, Guy's Hospital, and the Blue Coat Schools, all had Anglican support, and have bequeathed to us extensive records. For the history of an important charitable movement which had much Anglican involvement at both local and national levels, see:

• Jones, M.G. *The Charitable School Movement: a Study of Eighteenth Century Puritanism in Action*. (Cambridge University Press, 1938. Reprinted Frank Cass & Co., 1984).

The history of philanthropy is recounted in:

• Owen, David. *English Philanthropy, 1660-1960*. (Belknap Press of Harvard University, 1965).

An extensive list of Victorian charities active in London is provided by:

• Victorian London – Charities – list of charities
  www.victorianlondon.org/dickens/dickens-charities.htm

A. PARISH AND LOCAL CHARITIES

Charity was central to parish life, and modest benefactions abounded. Many parishes were responsible for the administration of local charities established by wealthy benefactors. Parish clergy, churchwardens and/or overseers were frequently named as trustees of such charities. Bishops frequently enquired about such charities in their visitation queries. Charities might be established to support the poor, conduct schools, apprentice children, pay clergy and engage in a wide range of other charitable activities. It was natural to ask incumbents and parish officers to accept responsibility for administering property bequeathed to support a charity. Their deeds, minutes and correspondence (which can frequently be found amongst parish records) may provide much information about parish life, and about the lives of both trustees and beneficiaries. Subscription lists frequently record the names of those who contributed towards the building of a new church or school, or helped to establish a charity. Charity boards, erected in churches in order to prevent endowments being lost, frequently give details of charitable donations received by the parish, naming donors. The records of schools run by parish officers may include details of schoolmasters and pupils. Apprenticeship charity indentures name apprentices, masters and trustees, and state the trades which were to be taught.[3] Charity Commission reports, which are frequently available in local record offices, provide detailed accounts of many parochial charities.

In the Year 1731. DAME MARGARET THOROLD WIDOW, and Relict of S.ʳ IOHN THOROLD; late of MARSTON BARR.ᵗ Transfer'd to S.ᵗ IOHN THOROLD, of this County BARR.ᵗ and IOHN THOROLD Esq.ʳ his Eldest Son; One Thousand Five Hundred Pounds, South Sea Annuities; in trust, to lay out the Money arifeing by the Sale thereof in the Purchafe of Lands of Inheritance in this County, the Rents, and Profits, of which, and the Produce of the Said Annuities till Sold, to be Equaly Divided Between Six Poor Old Men of the CITY and Minfter of LINCOLN, that are paft their Labour and do not Receive Alms of the Parifh, as more fully appears by a Deed bearing Date the 13.ᵗʰ

Day of Ianuary,

Regiftred in LINCOLN Minfter. the Lands are att Sturton: in the Parish of Stow, in this County,

Commemoration of a charity at Lincoln Cathedral.

B. NATIONAL CHARITIES

A handful of national Anglican charities date to the late seventeenth and eighteenth centuries, but many were founded in the nineteenth century. Their concerns ranged from evangelism to drink, from the support of impoverished clergy to the building of new churches. Many of our ancestors served as trustees or as employees; others benefited from their ministrations. This section includes brief notes on some of the major societies, together with an indication of where their archives can be found. Many had local branches or auxiliaries, which assisted with fund-raising and/or the distribution of literature. The records of such auxiliaries have frequently been deposited in local record offices, perhaps with parish records. Local record offices may also hold the archives of charitable societies which operated at diocesan or sub-diocesan level, for example, the Oxford Diocesan Church Building Society, or the Bedfordshire Necessitous Clergy Society.[4]

Additional Curates Society

This society was founded in 1837 with a donation of £500 from William IV. The Society assumed responsibility for paying the stipends of curates where the local parish could not afford to do so. By the late 1860s, it was sponsoring c.500 curates.[5]

Many letters and papers concerning the Society can be found in Lambeth Palace Library, and through the union catalogues listed above, pp.53–4. The records of parishes which were awarded grants by the Society may also contain relevant papers.

The Church Army

The Church Army was founded in 1882 by Wilson Carlisle in order to evangelize in the slums of Westminster. Its activities were endorsed by the Church of England, although Carlisle's use of his converts to evangelize their fellows was originally regarded with deep suspicion by some clergy. Conversely, he was able to attract many committed Christians who had become Nonconformists because they had been treated merely as pew fodder by the Establishment. The Army's work rapidly expanded, with the establishment of prison, caravan, tent and beach missions, homes for men and women, and a training college. During the two world wars, work with servicemen was important. Church Army evangelists continue to operate today.

Some archives are held by Cambridge University Library, although these are currently not fully catalogued, and restricted. Other records are still held by the Church Army. For a brief history, see:

- Church Army
  www.churcharmy.org.uk
  Click 'About Us', and 'Our History'.

The Church Lads' Brigade

The Church Lads' Brigade is the Church of England's uniformed youth organization. It was founded in 1891, in response to the growth of the Nonconformist Boys' Brigade movement. The Brigade's Historical Group has produced many fact sheets about its history, including lists of various officers, and a guide to 'The Brigade Archive'. Visit:

- Church Lads' and Church Girls' Brigade: Historical Group
  www.clcgb.org.uk/about-us/history

Local records of Brigade activities can frequently be found amongst parish records.

Church of England Mens' Society

A number of organizations joined together in 1899 to form the Church of England Men's Society, 'devoting itself to all kinds of work amongst men'. It had many parochial branches, but closed in 1985. Minutes and other records of its branches can frequently be found amongst parish records. The minutes and papers of its executive committee, 1899–1986, are held by Lambeth Palace Library.

Church of England Sunday School Institute

The purpose of this Institute, formed in 1843, was to meet the specific needs of Anglican Sunday School teachers. It was active in supporting them through publications and training. It merged with the National Society (see below) in 1935, and its records are held with that Society's archives in the Church of England Record Centre **www.lambethpalacelibrary.org/content/cerc**.

Church of England Temperance Society

Founded in 1862, this Society had its roots in the Anglo-Catholic movement, and had many local branches. It operated a number of homes for inebriates, and its volunteer Police Court Missionaries played a major role in founding the Probation Service. Since 1969 it has become a part of the Church of England Council for Social Aid. Its minutes and papers from 1880 are held by Lambeth Palace Library. Local branch papers can be identified in the union catalogues listed above, pp.53–4.

Church Pastoral Aid Society

This Society was founded in 1836 in order to increase the number of clergymen in the Church of England, and to encourage the appointment of pious and discreet laymen as helpers to the clergy in non-ministerial duties. Like the Additional Curates Society, it was sponsoring c.500 curates by the late 1860s.[6] Its archives, with those of a number of related organizations, are now held in the Cadbury Research Library at the University of Birmingham. They include the records of a number of local auxiliaries, which include much material of interest to local historians. Records of a number of other auxiliaries may be identified in the union catalogues listed above, pp.53–4. For a brief note on the Society's history, see:

- Church Pastoral Aid Society: History
  www.cpas.org.uk/about-CPAS/history

Clergy Orphan Corporation

The Corporation was established in 1749 to educate the orphaned children of the clergy, and ran separate schools for boys and girls. The register of its boys' school (known as St. Edmund's School since 1897) has been published:

- Simmonds, Mark John. *Register of the Clergy Orphan School for Boys, 1751-1896.* (Augustine's College, 1897).

The Corporation was amalgamated with the Corporation of the Sons of the Clergy (see below) in 1969. Relevant papers can be found in the Church of England Record Centre.

Corporation of the Sons of the Clergy
This institution was originally established in 1655, and incorporated in 1678, in order to assist loyal clergy and their dependents who had suffered during the Civil War and Interregnum. It supported impecunious and aged clergy and their widows, sent their children to school, and apprenticed orphans. Records held at London Metropolitan Archives include minutes, administrative papers, papers of associated charities, accounts, subscriptions, donations and bequests, estate papers, etc. A variety of other sources are listed in Cox's history of the Corporation:

• Cox, Nicholas. *Bridging the Gap: A History of the Corporation of the Sons of the Clergy Over 300 Years, 1655-1978*. (Becket Pubns, 1978).
• Pearce, E.H. *The Sons of the Clergy 1655-1904*. (John Murray, 1904).

Curates' Augmentation Fund
This fund was established in 1866 in order to increase the incomes of assistant curates, whose numbers had rapidly increased in the preceding decades. The Fund aimed to assist curates who had remained unbeneficed for more than fifteen years. Lambeth Palace Library holds some records; others can be found through the union catalogues listed above (pp.53–4).

English Church Union
This Union is an Anglo-Catholic advocacy group, originally founded in 1859 as the Church of England Protection Society. Since 1933 it has been called the Church Union. Its archives are held by Lambeth Palace Library. Various documents relating to it can be found at:

• Project Canterbury: English Church Union
  http://anglicanhistory.org/england/ecu

For a brief history, see:

• A History of the Church Union
  www.churchunion.co.uk/history.php

Girls' Friendly Society

This society was formed at Lambeth Palace in 1875 to support working-class girls who had left home in order to find work in urban centres. It established many hostels. By 1900, it had over 150,000 Members and nearly 33,000 Associates in 1,361 branches. Its members were mainly domestic servants, although others were teachers, nurses, clerks, students and workers in refreshment bars, mills, factories and warehouses. For an outline of its history, see:

• Girls' Friendly Society: Our History
  http://girlsfriendlysociety.org.uk/history.html

The Society's central archives are deposited in the Women's Library at the London School of Economics, and are listed in its catalogue **http://twl-calm.library.lse.ac.uk/CalmView/**. Many of its branch records, which include membership registers, minutes, reports and other documents, are deposited in local record offices.

Incorporated Church Building Society

The role of this Society was to encourage the building of new churches. It was established in 1818 as the Society for Promoting the Building and Enlargement of Churches and Chapels, but was re-named in 1828. By 1868, it had disbursed almost £600,000 in grants towards the building of new churches and the expansion or re-building of old ones.[7] Boards recording its support, and its ban on renting pews, can be seen in many churches. Its archives, which date from 1818 to 1982, are held by Lambeth Palace Library. They include plans of 12,000 churches which it helped fund. There are also files for each church, which may include correspondence, subscription lists, photographs and other information. Minutes of the Society record the progress of grant applications. The plans have been digitized, and were formerly available online. They will probably be made available again soon after this book is published. For more information, see:

• Using Church Plans Online to access the Incorporated Church Building Society (ICBS) Archive
www.lambethpalacelibrary.org/files/using_the_icbs_ archive_0.pdf

Mothers' Union
In 1876, Mary Sumner, wife of a vicar, began the movement which came to be known as the Mothers' Union. Her aim was to enable mothers to support one another, and to train them in motherhood. The movement spread rapidly. The Mothers' Union Central Council was formed in 1896, and attracted the patronage of Queen Victoria; by the turn of the century there were 169,000 members. Members signed a card and were 'enrolled'; minutes, registers and other documents sometimes survive amongst parish and diocesan records in local record offices.

The central archives are held by Lambeth Palace Library. A detailed history, together with biographical notes on past presidents and an extensive bibliography, is provided by:

• Moyse, Cordelia. *A History of the Mothers' Union: Women, Anglicanism and Globalisation, 1876-2008.* (Boydell Press, 2009).

National Society
Education was a priority for most Anglican clergy, who actively promoted schools; many actually taught in them. Handbooks for clergy regarded schools as 'the most powerful and excellent organ of parish life and village work'.[8] The clergy's educational activities were greatly assisted when the National Society for Promoting the Education of the Poor in the Principles of the Established Church throughout England and Wales was founded in 1817. Its aim was to

establish a Church of England school in every parish. The aim was never fully accomplished, although many of the 5,000 church schools currently in operation were founded by the Society. The Society's archives include c.10,000 parish files covering every school it considered for a grant. Applications for grants provide much information on matters such as accommodation, numbers of pupils and other local schools. Much financial information is also provided

A National School in Lincoln.

Look out for datestones like this.

in these files. The Society's annual reports are also very detailed. In the 1830s and 1840s they included a number of surveys of school provision. The *Church School Inquiry 1846/7*, published in 1849, is a national survey of provision by parish. Similar surveys in summarised format were published again in 1856–7 and 1866–7.

For a brief introduction to the history of the society, see:

• Chalk to Mouse: The story of the National Society for the Promotion of the Education of the Poor in the Principles of the Established Church, and some of its schools **www.soundarchitect.org.uk/wp-content/uploads/2012/10/SA_chalkmouse_PDF_v6a.pdf**

More detailed histories include:

- Burgess, Henry James. *Enterprise in Education: The story of the work of the Established Church in the education of the people prior to 1870.* (National Society/S.P.C.K, 1958).
- Burgess, H.J., and Welsby, P.A. *A Short History of the National Society, 1811-1961.* (National Society, 1961).
- Loudon, Lois. *Distinctive and Inclusive: The National Society and Church of England Schools, 1811–2011.* (National Society, 2011). Online at **www.churchofengland.org/media/2483039/nshistory.pdf**. This includes a useful up-to-date bibliography identifying sources.

The archives of the Society[9] are discussed in:

- Lambeth Palace Library & Church of England Record Centre Research Guide: Education Sources **www.lambethpalacelibrary.org/files/Education_0.pdf**

Society for the Promotion of Christian Knowledge
The S.P.C.K. was founded by Thomas Bray, a Church of England clergyman, in 1699.[10] Its aim was to promote popular education. It encouraged the foundation of many eighteenth-century charity schools and parish libraries, was a pioneer in teacher education, and was also the major publisher of Christian literature in eighteenth- and nineteenth-century Britain. In the provinces, corresponding members helped to establish schools and distribute its literature.

The Society's national archives, including minutes, annual reports, accounts, correspondence (mostly eighteenth-century) etc., are held by Cambridge University Library. Early printed *Accounts* record brief details of the schools supported. The papers of local schools and committees can frequently be found in local record offices; these might include minutes of the governors, registers, apprenticeship records, accounts, lists of subscribers and other miscellaneous documents.[11]

Some early minutes of the Society, which give the names of many members, are in print:

- Clement, Mary, ed. *Correspondence and Minutes of the S.P.C.K. relating to Wales 1699-1740.* (University of Wales Press, 1952).
- McClure, Edmund, ed. *A chapter in English church history: being the minutes of the Society for Promoting Christian Knowledge for the years 1698-1704, together with abstracts of correspondents' letters during part of the same period.* (S.P.C.K. Tract Committee, 1888).

The history of the Society is recounted in:

- Allen, W.O.B., and McClure, E. *Two Hundred Years: the History of the Society for Promoting Christian Knowledge, 1698-1898.* (Society for Promoting Christian Knowledge, 1898).
- Clarke, W. Lowther. *A History of the S.P.C.K.* (S.P.C.K., 1959).

For a discussion of the Society's membership (which included many corresponding members in the provinces), see:

- Bultmann, William A., and Bultmann, Phyllis W. 'The Roots of Anglican Humanitarianism: a study of the membership of the S.P.C.K. and S.P.G.', *Historical Magazine of the Protestant Episcopal Church* 33(1) (1964), pp.3–48.

Society for the Relief of Poor Clergymen
This Society was founded in 1788 in order to assist distressed clergyman and their dependants. It is still in operation today. Records at Lambeth Palace Library comprise minute books and registers, 1788–1864.

Waifs and Strays Society
In 1881, Edward De Montjoie Rudolf, a Sunday School teacher in South Lambeth, founded this society in order to provide homes for destitute children. By 1905 3,410 children were in its care, and it had

93 homes scattered across England and Wales. Its name has changed on several occasions; in 1946 it became the 'Church of England Children's Society', and is now known (since 1982) as 'The Children's Society'. It no longer runs homes.

The Children's Society maintains its own archives, which consist primarily of 140,000 case files for individual children assisted by the Society. The archives also include publicity material, photographs, supporters' magazines and many other types of material. They are fully catalogued at:

- The Children's Society Archive
  www.calmview.eu/childrensociety/Calmview/

For a brief history of the Society, with some anonymized files, visit:

- Hidden Lives Revealed: a Virtual Archive: Children in Care 1881–1981
  www.hiddenlives.org.uk

C. MISSIONARY SOCIETIES

The Church has always been interested in mission. However, the evangelical revival of the eighteenth and nineteenth centuries prompted more serious thought about how to spread the message of the Gospel overseas. It also prompted action, although the number of missionaries remained low until the 1880s. There were perhaps c.9,000 British missionaries active overseas in 1900.[12]

Mission required organization, and most denominations formed missionary societies. There were also a number of non-denominational societies. With one exception, only those societies which were solely Anglican will be considered here. For useful introductions to the history of missionary activities, see:

- Porter, Andrew. *Religion versus Empire? British Protestant Missionaries and Overseas Expansion, 1790-1914.* (Manchester University Press, 2004).

• Stanley, B. *The Bible and the Flag: Protestant Missions and British Imperialism in the Nineteenth and twentieth centuries*. (Apollos, 1990).

Missionary society archives provide much information concerning missionaries and their work, and about the support they received from local churches and congregations in England. Parish records may provide information about local supporters of societies. Individual missionaries were frequently linked to specific parishes who provided financial and spiritual support.

Many missionary societies have deposited their archives in record offices. The largest multi-denominational collection of missionary archives in the UK is held by the School of Oriental and African Studies (SOAS) **www.soas.ac.uk/library/archives/collections/ missionary-collections**. A detailed union catalogue of over 400 collections is provided by:

• Mundus: Gateway to Missionary Collections in the UK **www.mundus.ac.uk**

For an older survey of missionary archives, see:

• Keen, Rosemary. *A Survey of the Archives of Selected Missionary Societies*. (Historical Manuscripts Commission, 1968).

British and Foreign Bible Society
This non-denominational society was founded in 1804 in order to make bibles in Welsh easily available. It was inspired by the story of Mary Jones, who saved for six years and then walked 26 miles across rugged country to buy a bible in her own language. When Joseph Hughes brought her journey to the attention of the Religious Tract Society, members of the Clapham Sect (including William Wilberforce) took action, and established this Society to promote the distribution of bibles. During the First World War over 9,000,000 bibles in 90 different languages were distributed.

The Society's archives are held by Cambridge University Library. They include detailed annual reports, minutes of various committees, and incoming letters, many of which are arranged by the names of correspondents. The latter included, for instance, translators, overseas agents and supporters in the UK. Some records of local auxiliaries, including minutes, and sometimes lists of subscribers, are deposited with the Society's archives; others may sometimes be found in local archives.

- Canton, William. *A History of the British and Foreign Bible Society*. (5 vols. John Murray, 1904–1910). Vol. 2 includes a list of committee members to 1854; this is continued in Vol. 5, which also lists some officers.
- Roe, James Moulton. *A History of the British and Foreign Bible Society 1905-1954*. (British & Foreign Bible Society, 1965).

Church Missionary Society

The Church Missionary Society was founded in 1799. By 1896, it had 903 missionaries working overseas.[13] Its early missionaries (before the 1860s) were required to compile quarterly journals of their day-to-day activities, which are now amongst the Society's archives. They were replaced by summary reports known as 'annual letters'. 'Mission books' contain copies of both the early journals, and of all the in-letters received by the Society. Other archives, including applications to become missionaries, a 'Register of Missionaries 1804–1918', minutes, out-letters, and financial records, are now held by Birmingham University's Cadbury Research Library, and described by:

- University of Birmingham Archives and Manuscripts Collections **www.birmingham.ac.uk/facilities/cadbury/archives/ index.aspx**
Click 'Records of the Church Missionary Society'

Much of the collection has been digitized. See:

- Church Missionary Society Archive: General Introduction and Guide to the Archive
  www.ampltd.co.uk/digital_guides/church_missionary_ society_archive_general

See also:

- Cobb, Henry S. 'The Archives of the Church Missionary Society', *Archives* 2(14) (1955), pp.293–9.
- Keen, Rosemary. 'The Church Missionary Society Archives: or thirty years work in the basement', *Catholic Archives*, 12 (1992), pp.21–31.

Many C.M.S. periodicals have been digitized:

- Adam Matthew: Church Missionary Society Periodicals
  www.amdigital.co.uk/m-collections/collection/church-missionary-society-periodicals

The Society's history is recounted by:

- Hewitt, Gordon. *The Problems of Success: a History of the Church Missionary Society 1910-1942*. (2 vols. S.C.M. Press, 1971–7).

An older work includes detailed accounts of the work of many individual missionaries:

- Stock, Eugene. *The History of the Church Missionary Society: its Environment, its Men, and its Work*. (4 vols. C.M.S., 1899–1916).

Society for the Propagation of the Gospel in Foreign Parts
This Society, now known as the United Society, was formed in 1701 as a sister society to the Society for the Promotion of Christian Knowledge (see above, pp.165–6), and its early membership was very

similar. Its original purpose was to provide the American colonists with clergy, and also to send missionaries to work amongst slaves and the indigenous population. In 1825, it took over the sponsorship of missionaries hitherto supported by the S.P.C.K.[14] Its work subsequently extended to the West Indies, to other British colonies, and, in the mid-nineteenth century, to countries such as China and Japan. In 1896, it had 612 overseas missionaries.[15] For modern histories of the Society, see:

- Glasson, T. *Mastering Christianity: Missionary Anglicanism and Slavery in the Atlantic World*. (Oxford University Press, 2012).
- O'Connor, Daniel, et al. *Three Centuries of Mission: the United Society for the Propagation of the Gospel*. (Continuum, 2000).

Much more biographical information, including a 'summary of the missionary roll, 1701–1900', is provided in:

- Pascoe, C.F. *Two Hundred Years of the SPG: an historical account of the Society for the Propagation of the Gospel In Foreign parts, 1701-1900 (based on a digest of the Society's Records)*. (USPG, 1901).

The Society's archives are held by the Bodleian Library, Oxford, and by Lambeth Palace Library. For the Bodleian collection, see:

- Bodleian Library: Collection Level Description: Papers of the United Society for the Propagation of the Gospel **www.bodley.ox.ac.uk/dept/scwmss/wmss/online/blcas/ uspg.html**

Some eighteenth-century papers are held by Lambeth Palace Library. The names of numerous British and overseas correspondents are listed in:

- Manross, William Wilson. *S.P.G. Papers in the Lambeth Palace Library: Calendar and Indexes*. (Clarendon Press, 1974).

Universities' Mission to Central Africa

This mission was founded in 1857 in order to follow up on David Livingstone's work. It played an important role in opposing the slave trade, and in the fight against leprosy. It is now part of the United Society (see above), and its archives are held in the Bodleian Library at Oxford.

For the history of the Society, see:

• Anderson-Morshead, A.E.M. *The History of the Universities' Mission to Central Africa*. (3 vols. The Mission, 1955). Vol. 1. 1859–99. Vol. 2. 1907–32. Vol. 3. 1933–57.
• Wilson, George Herbert. *The History of the Universities' Mission to Central Africa*. (The Mission, 1936).

D. RELIGIOUS ORDERS

Religious orders in the established church were abolished in England by Henry VIII, and not re-established until the nineteenth century. Under the influence of the Tractarian movement, more than ninety communities for women were established between 1845 and 1900. An estimated 10,000 women joined them. There were far fewer communities for men. Eighteen male communities were founded in the same period, but only seven survived in 1900, although a few had transferred allegiance to the Church of Rome.[16] In the nineteenth century, the sisterhoods offered opportunities for women in social work, in teaching, and in nursing, which were not easily found elsewhere.

Most of the women's orders were dedicated to working amongst the poor. They had the advantage over the clergy that they really did live in poverty themselves; they deliberately set out to match the lifestyles of the poor, rather than to create outposts of middle-class affluence in poor neighbourhoods.

A brief historical account of each Anglican community founded between 1845 and 1955 is provided by:

• Anson, P.F. *The Call of the Cloister: Religious Communities and Kindred Bodies in the Anglican Communion*. (S.P.C.K., 1955).

The nineteenth-century origins of these communities are discussed by:

- Allchin, A.M. *The Silent Rebellion: Anglican Religious Communities, 1845-1900*. (S.C.M. Press, 1958).

For a valuable discussion of Anglican sisterhoods, see:

- Mumm, Susan. *Stolen Daughters, Virgin Mothers: Anglican Sisterhoods in Victorian Britain*. (Leicester University Press, 1999).

Most communities still hold their own archives, although it may be worth checking the union catalogues mentioned on pp.53–4. Relevant papers are also held by Lambeth Palace Library, and by Pusey House. Mumm's book includes a useful guide to sources.

Chapter 10

TRACING ANGLICAN CLERGY

A. INTRODUCTION; THE CLERGY OF THE CHURCH OF ENGLAND DATABASE

Most of the sources discussed in previous chapters provide information about Anglican clergymen. For example, both parish registers and bishops' transcripts were signed by incumbents. However, clergy are most easily traced through the records that were kept of significant milestones in their careers. Their education, their ordination, and their institutions to their livings, all left records. So did a variety of other events in their careers, such as appointment to curacies, and death.

Many of these sources have been abstracted for a major database listing Anglican clergy, covering the period 1540–1835. The Clergy of the Church of England Database **http://theclergydatabase. org.uk** lists most (but not all) major events in clerical careers, including ordinations, licensings, institutions and resignations. It also frequently includes details of patronage. This database is derived from numerous sources found in diocesan archives, which will be described below. However, it does not include information from University registers. Probate records and bishops' transcripts are sometimes abstracted, but not always. Parish records have not been consulted, nor are the records of clerical taxation held by the National Archives abstracted.

B. CLERICAL EDUCATION

The majority of post-Reformation clergy attended one of the universities, and are therefore listed in university registers. These provide the principal source for the social origins of clergymen, and frequently include information relating to students' later career'. They are omitted from CCEd (as we shall refer to the database). Diocesan records do sometimes note colleges attended and degrees obtained, and such information may be recorded by CCEd, but for more detailed information it is necessary to consult the printed registers, which are available online at **https://archive.org** and on other websites, as well as in hard copy:

- Foster, Joseph. *Alumni Oxonienses 1500-1886.* (8 vols. James Parker & Co., 1887–92. Reprinted in 4 vols., Kraus Reprint, 1980). Not as accurate as it should be.
- Foster, Joseph. *Oxford Men 1880-1892, with a record of their Schools, Honors and Degrees.* (James Parker & Co., 1893).
- Venn, J., & Venn, J.A. *Alumni Cantabrigienses.* Pt. 1. [1500]–1751 (4 vols). Pt 2. 1751–1900 (6 vols. Cambridge University Press, 1922–54).

There are also many biographical dictionaries for the separate Oxbridge colleges. A few other universities have published similar lists of their alumni. In England, these included Durham and London. Some Anglicans studied at Aberdeen, Edinburgh, Glasgow and St. Andrews (Scotland), and Dublin (Ireland).

A small number of degrees were awarded by the Archbishop of Canterbury. See:

- Lambeth Palace Library Research Guide: List of Lambeth degrees (by name) **www.lambethpalacelibrary.org/files/lambeth_degrees_name_1.pdf**

In the early nineteenth century, preparation for ordination usually consisted of attendance at a dozen or so university lectures, plus the reading of a few theological works. Ordinands had to be at least 23. Younger men might spend a year or so studying in the home of a clergyman. In 1857, James Anderson, rector of Tormarton

(Gloucestershire) hoped to train six ordinands, and receive fees of £200 from each of them.[1]

After 1850, Oxbridge graduates were beginning to lose their dominance amongst the clergy, as the demand for pastoral and sacerdotal skills amongst ordinands increased. By the 1890s, roughly a quarter had been trained in non-graduate theological colleges.[2] In the 1960s, twenty-six Anglican theological colleges were at work.[3] Their archives are likely to include details of both staff and students: applications, registers, testimonials and other records. The archives of a few colleges can be noted here. The earliest was St. Bees (Cumberland), founded in 1816 and closed in 1895. Its archives are held by Cumbria Archive Service. For its history, see:

• Park, Trevor. *St Bees College, Pioneering Higher Education in 19th Century Cumbria*. (St Bega Publications, 2008).

Cuddesdon College was founded in 1854. It merged with Ripon Hall in the 1970s, and is now known as Ripon College Cuddesdon. For its history, see:

• Chadwick, Owen. *The Founding of Cuddesdon*. (Oxford University Press, 1954).
• Chapman, Mark D., ed. *Ambassadors of Christ: Commemorating 150 Years of Theological Education in Cuddesdon 1854–2004*. (Ashgate, 2004).

The evangelical London College of Divinity was founded in 1863 in order to train men whose educational background meant they were unable to attend Oxford or Cambridge. It moved to Nottingham in 1969, changing its name to St John's College. Its archives, including papers relating to staff appointments and student enrolment, are now held by the Cadbury Research Library at the University of Birmingham **www.birmingham.ac.uk/facilities/cadbury**. For its history, see:

- Davies, G.C.B. *College Men for the Ministry: The History of the London College of Divinity*. (Hodder & Stoughton, 1963).

Westcott House was founded in 1881 as the Cambridge Clergy Training School. It holds its own archives.

The Society of the Sacred Mission was founded in 1893, and opened Kelham Hall as its training college from 1903. It closed in 1972. Its archives, including some details of students, are held by the Borthwick Institute **https://borthcat.york.ac.uk/index.php/society-of-sacred-mission-archive**.

The College of the Resurrection, popularly known as Mirfield, was founded in 1903. Its archives are also held by the Borthwick Institute **https://borthcat.york.ac.uk/index.php/mirfield-papers**.

Much information on all theological colleges is provided by:

- Bullock, F.W.B. *A History of Training for the Ministry of the Church of England in England and Wales from 1800 to 1874*. (Budd & Gillatt, 1955). A further volume covers *1875–1974* (Home Words Printing & Publishing, 1976).

For a more general history of theological training institutions, see:

- Dowland, David A. *Nineteenth-Century Anglican Theological Training: the Redbrick Challenge*. (Clarendon Press, 1997).

C. THE CLERGY CAREER PATH

Men (and only men!) wishing to join the clergy had first to be ordained by a bishop as a deacon, and, subsequently, as a priest. The diaconal year was regarded as a period of probation. Many ordinands with a title (evidence of financial support) in one diocese sought *letters dimissory* from its bishop if they wished to be ordained elsewhere. Many of these letters can be found in diocesan archives (but not necessarily in CCEd). Numbers decreased in the nineteenth century, as travel became easier.

Until the nineteenth century, if a candidate had the requisite title, a degree and the appropriate testimonial, bishops felt unable to refuse ordination. From c.1800, however, candidates faced increasingly searching examinations by bishops before ordination. Ordinands had to provide a certificate that their intention to seek holy orders had been announced in their parish church, testimonials from local clergymen and college tutors,[4] proof of age (usually a baptismal certificate – see above, pp.86–7), and proof that they possessed a curacy, benefice, college fellowship or other means of subsistence. From the early twentieth century, printed forms provide detailed information on candidates' parentage, education and reasons for applying for orders. From the late nineteenth century, there may also be reports from incumbents on ordinands officiating as curates during their year's diaconate. All of these documents (until 1835) can be found amongst ordination papers in diocesan archives, although they may not be in CCEd. Ordinations were formally recorded in diocesan registers, which are in CCEd. When a see was vacant, ordinations, institutions and other episcopal acts were conducted by the appropriate archbishop, and must be sought in his registers (also covered by CCEd).

Many clergymen began their careers by taking a curacy. Some never advanced beyond that stage. Indeed, in the late sixteenth century few who served as curates subsequently gained incumbencies; there were two distinct and rarely overlapping groups, the beneficed and the unbeneficed clergy.[5] Serving a curacy was not at this time seen as an essential qualification for an incumbent.

In the ensuing centuries, there were more opportunities for curates to advance. However, the dramatic nineteenth-century growth in the number of ordinands, which was not matched by any significant increase in the number of benefices, again meant that many failed to obtain a benefice. Approximately a fifth of Cambridge graduates ordained between 1800 and 1830 served as unbeneficed curates throughout their careers.[6] They were, in practice, the workhorses of the church.

Many pre-nineteenth century curates were in sole charge of their parishes, serving on behalf of a non-resident clergyman. That began to change after the Pluralities Acts of 1838 and 1850 severely restricted the ability of incumbents to be non-resident. Curates could therefore no longer take sole charge of their parishes; that had to be the incumbent's role. Many, however, were needed to serve as assistant curates, especially in large urban parishes such as Leeds. Service as a curate was increasingly seen as essential training for a clergyman before institution to a benefice; indeed, today most curates are in training.

Curates had to be licensed by the bishop; their names are recorded in licensing books, together with those of schoolmasters, surgeons, and midwives (see pp.131–7). After the Stipendiary Curates Act of 1813, bishops decided the stipends of curates in sole charge of parishes (although not of assistant curates). Unemployment and low pay, however, were issues for many clergymen; hence the need for some of the charities mentioned in Chapter 9.

Many clergy served as schoolmasters, either before they were ordained, or whilst they held an incumbency. Schoolmasters in endowed grammar schools were primarily clergy. Many clergymen taught privately, or conducted schools in their own parishes, sometimes voluntarily. Clergy who were schoolmasters required schoolmasters' licences (see pp.135–7).

After ordination, clergymen sought patrons willing to present them to a bishop for institution to a parochial benefice. If bishops themselves owned advowsons, candidates were collated rather than instituted. Institution or collation took place privately, frequently in the bishop's palace. The ordinary would then issue a mandate for induction to the archdeacon, or perhaps induct the candidate himself. Induction took place in the parish church. The new incumbent was presented to his parishioners; the glebe, the parsonage, the tithes, and any other rights, were formally handed over to him. Institution registers are likely to record the date of institution, the name of the patron, by whom the candidate was instituted, and the reason why the living was vacant.

If the living was in the gift of the Crown, there should be a record of presentation on the patent rolls in The National Archives, class C 66. These run from 1201 to 1946; many have been calendared. See:

• Royal grants: letters patent and charters from 1199
  **www.nationalarchives.gov.uk/records/research-guides/
  royal-grants.htm**

If the candidate was the son of the previous incumbent, he needed a dispensation from the Archbishop, in order to prevent any idea that the living had become hereditary. Dispensations could also be obtained to receive the orders of deacon and priest together, to be ordained under-age, or to hold benefices in plurality. These dispensations are recorded in the Archbishops' act books in Lambeth Palace Library, and are indexed in:

• Dunkin, Edwin Hadlow Wise, et al, eds. *Index to the Act books of
  the Archbishops of Canterbury. 1663-1859.* (Index Library 55 & 63.
  British Record Society, 1929–38).

Various records of ordinations and institutions compiled for the Archbishops of Canterbury are held by Lambeth Palace Library. In 1665, Archbishop Sheldon required bishops to make an annual return of the names, titles, degrees and orders of all persons ordained.[7] The order was repeated on various occasions in the late seventeenth and early eighteenth centuries. Returns for a few dioceses are still amongst the Vicar Generals' archives. The Library also holds a register of ordinands, arranged by dioceses, with notes of those refused orders, 1694–1704.

Clergy who had been ordained and inducted to a living can be traced through visitation records, especially the call books (see pp.108–10). These books frequently record details of ordinations, appointments, and dispensations, and are included in CCEd.

Once a clergyman had been instituted to a rectory or vicarage, the living became his freehold, and he could not be removed easily.

However, a patron who intended to present his son to a living when he was old enough sometimes used the device of the resignation bond to ensure that the living would be vacant at the right time. Livings could not be kept vacant for more than six months; otherwise, the bishop was entitled to fill the vacancy himself. Patrons sometimes, therefore, had to make a presentation before the person they wished to present was of age. Resignation bonds provided a means of escaping the dilemma. The clergyman seeking patronage would enter a bond to vacate the living when required, or forfeit a substantial sum of money. Resignation bonds may sometimes be found amongst family and estate papers.[8] Their use was abolished in 1898.

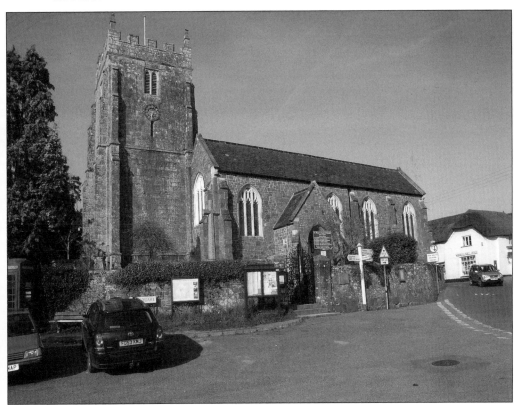

Whimple in Devon – a nineteenth-century church built in traditional style.

The pulpit at Tormarton in Gloucestershire.

D. CLERGY SUBSCRIPTIONS AND OATHS

At the time of their ordination and appointment, clergy had to subscribe to various doctrinal and political statements. In 1559, both clergy and lay public officers had to take the Oath of Supremacy recognizing Elizabeth I's status as 'supreme governor'. Since 1571, they have all had to accept the Thirty-Nine Articles. After the Restoration, they all had to make declarations disavowing the Solemn League and Covenant, asserting the illegality of taking up arms against the Crown, and assenting to the *Book of Common Prayer*. Those who refused were ejected from their livings. Clergy subscriptions and oaths are recorded in subscription books (included in CCEd), and provide another means to trace them. For a subscription book in print, see:

• Williams, Barrie, ed. *The Subscription Book of Bishops Tounson and Davenant, 1620-1640*. (Wiltshire Record Society, 32. 1977).

See also:

• Carter, E.H. *The Norwich Subscription Books: a study of the subscription books of the Diocese of Norwich, 1637-1800*. (T. Nelson & Son, 1937).

E. CLERICAL TAXATION

Newly-appointed medieval clergy had to pay a proportion of their first year's income, known as first fruits, to the Pope. Thereafter, they also had to pay a notional tenth of their annual income. After the Reformation, these taxes became due to the Crown, although vicarages valued at under £10, and rectories valued at less than £6 13s 4d, were exempted. After 1704 the revenue was allocated to Queen Anne's Bounty (see Section F below), and used to augment the incomes of poorer benefices. The tax was abolished in 1926. Records are now in The National Archives. Bishops had to certify institutions to the Exchequer; their certificates are in E 331. Other records are in E 332-344, E 347, and QAB 1.

In 1534, when first fruits and tenths were first transferred to the Crown, a major survey of church property was undertaken to determine what sums were payable. The incomes of all parochial benefices, as well as that of cathedrals, monasteries, colleges, etc., was recorded. This survey remained the basis of first fruits taxation until 1926, despite the huge subsequent increases in the incomes of many benefices. The returns are now in The National Archives, class E 344, although some from the Dioceses of London, Ely, and York, and also the counties of Berkshire, Rutland and Northumberland, are missing. Those which survive are printed in:

• *Valor Ecclesiasticus, temp. Henr. VIII. auctoritate regia institutus.* (6 vols. Record Commissioners, 1810).

Some information from the *Valor* (including from the missing returns) was abstracted in:

• Ecton, John. *Liber valorum & decimarum, being an account of such ecclesiastical benefices in England and Wales, as now stand charged with, or lately were discharged from the payment of first-fruits and tenths.* (1723). Several later editions.

It was not until 1835 that there was another attempt to value benefices. The *Values of Livings* were surveyed by the Ecclesiastical Commissioners, and published as a Parliamentary Paper.[9]

In addition to first fruits and tenths, the clergy were assessed for subsidies and poll taxes separately from the laity until 1664 (except between 1641 and 1660). The right of Convocation to grant clerical taxation was surrendered to Parliament in 1664 in order to avoid a revaluation of benefices, which would have exposed them to demands for higher first fruits and tenths.[10] Many records relating to clerical subsidies and poll taxes, and naming clergy, survive in the National Archives. These are listed at:

• E 179 Database
  www.nationalarchives.gov.uk/e179

For a detailed guide to clerical taxation records, see:

• Jurkowski, Maureen. 'The History of Clerical Taxation in England and Wales, 1173-1663: the findings of the E179 Project', *Journal of Ecclesiastical History* 76(1), 2016, pp.53–70.

F. QUEEN ANNE'S BOUNTY

Queen Anne's Bounty was originally established in 1704 to augment the incomes of poorer clergy. It was funded by first fruits and tenths (see above). Between 1809 and 1820, Parliament made annual grants to support the Bounty's work. Livings chosen for augmentation were chosen by ballot. The fund was originally used to purchase land for livings valued at less than £80 per year; the land purchased was generally worth c.£200. Increasingly, however, the moneys granted were left on deposit with the Bounty, which paid a moderate rate of interest. In 1829, it held £1,000,000 on deposit; by 1900 it held over £7,000,000. In 1947, the Bounty was merged with the Ecclesiastical Commissioners to form the Church Commissioners.

Relevant information can frequently be found amongst the parish records of augmented benefices. Conveyances of land purchased by the Bounty and given to parishes are enrolled on the Close Rolls, now in the National Archives, class C 54. The history of the Bounty is recounted in:

• Best, G.F.A. *Temporal Pillars: Queen Anne's Bounty, the Ecclesiastical Commission, and the Church of England.* (Cambridge University Press, 1964).

G. DEANS AND CANONS

Deans and canons of cathedrals and other capitular bodies were appointed in a variety of ways. Capitular archives are likely to include files of the documents produced when they were installed. For deans, these are likely to include letters recommendatory from the Crown, details of those who took part in elections, episcopal confirmations of elections, and episcopal mandates for their installation. Similar files are likely to be available for canons.

H. THE CIVIL WAR AND INTERREGNUM
During the Civil War and Interregnum, episcopal administration was in abeyance. The Church was under the authority of a range of Parliamentary committees and trustees. Many of their records were deposited with the Archbishop of Canterbury at the Restoration, and are now in Lambeth Palace Library. These include presentation deeds, institution papers, and registers of presentations, amongst much more.

After 1654, new ministers were vetted by the Committee for the Approbation of Public Preachers, or 'Triers'. Cromwell also established a range of local committees for the 'ejection of scandalous ministers'. Poor ministers were eligible for augmentations of their livings from the funds raised by the sale of episcopal lands (see below, pp.199–200). Records are listed in:

• Houston, Jane. *Catalogue of Ecclesiastical Records of the Commonwealth 1643-1660 in the Lambeth Palace Library* (Gregg International, 1968).

The Parliamentary Committee for Scandalous Ministers ejected those Royalists who it felt were not up to scratch, but gradually found itself assisting those who had suffered from the Royalists, and changed its name to the Committee for Plundered Ministers. Its records are in The National Archives, class SP 22. It operated through local committees; for an edition of the casebook of one of these, recording the charges brought by Suffolk parishioners against 'ill-affected' clergy, see:

• Holmes, Clive, ed. *Suffolk Committees for Scandalous Ministers 1644-46.* (Suffolk Records Society 13. 1970).

Despite the fact that bishops lost their authority during the Interregnum, some of them continued to ordain new priests. It has been calculated that perhaps 2,500 priests were ordained by them between 1646 and 1660. This activity is discussed by:

- Fincham, Kenneth, and Taylor, Stephen. 'Vital statistics: Episcopal Ordination and Ordinands in England, 1646-1660', *English Historical Review* 126(519) (2011), pp.319–44.

During the Civil War, many clergymen found themselves under the power of the party which they opposed, and were ejected from their livings. Two works give details of several thousand clergy ejected from their livings during and after the Civil War. Royalist clergy who suffered during the Great Rebellion are listed in:

- Matthews, A.G., ed. *Walker Revised, being a revision of John Walker's Sufferings of the Clergy during the Great Rebellion, 1642-60.* (Clarendon Press, 1948). A full name index is provided separately: Surman, C.E. *A.G. Matthew's Walker revised: supplementary index of intruders and others.* Occasional paper 2. (Dr. Williams's Library, 1956).

The clergy ejected after the Restoration are listed in:

- Matthews, A.G., ed. *Calamy Revised, being a revision of Edmund Calamy's Account of the ministers and others ejected and silenced, 1660-1662.* (Clarendon Press, 1934).

The claims made in these two works, and the sources used, are discussed by:

- Green, I. 'The Persecution of "Scandalous" and "Malignant" Clergy during the English Civil War', *English Historical Review*, 94 (1979), pp.507–31.

I. BIOGRAPHICAL WORKS

A variety of other listings and biographical dictionaries of clergy are available. Perhaps the most ubiquitous are the boards listing rectors and vicars which can now be seen in most churches, and which began to be erected in the late nineteenth century.

These of course can only be viewed *in situ* (and are not always accurate). Many other lists are in print. For senior diocesan and cathedral clergy, see:

• Fasti Ecclesiae Anglicana
  www.british-history.ac.uk/search/series/fasti-ecclesiae
  This is also available in a printed edition: Le Neve, John. *Fasti Ecclesiae Anglicanae, 1541-1867*. (11 vols. Athlone Press, 1969–2004). There are also modern multi-volume sets for 1066–1300 and 1300–1540.

A biographical dictionary of Protestants exiled for their beliefs during the reign of Queen Mary is provided by:

• Garrett, Christina Hallowell. *Marian Exiles: a study in the origin of Elizabethan Puritanism*. (Cambridge University Press, 1938).

Lists of clergy from many dioceses, together with Puritan comments on their suitability for office, are included in:

• Peel, Albert, ed. *The Seconde Parte of a Registers, being a calendar of manuscripts under that titled intended for publication by the Puritans about 1593 . . ..* (Cambridge University Press, 1915).

A list of non-jurors is included in:

• Overton, J.H. *The Non-Jurors: their Lives, Principles, and Writings*. (Smith, Elder, & Co., 1902).

Between 1817 and 1836, there were several not very accurate editions (with variant titles) of:

- *The Clerical Guide or ecclesiastical directory, containing a complete register of the prelates and other dignitaries of the church, a list of all the benefices in England and Wales . . . the names of their respective incumbents . . . .* (F.C. & J. Rivington, 1817–36).

A biographical dictionary of clergy in the period 1800–40 is provided in:

- Foster, Joseph. *Index ecclesiasticus . . . .* (Parker & Co., 1890).

After 1858, the easiest way to identify clergy is to consult the brief biographical notices in the irregularly-issued volumes of:

- *Crockford's Clerical Directory.* (Church House Publishing, 1858–).

Some twentieth-century volumes of Crockford's are now searchable by subscribers online at **www.crockford.org.uk**. There are a number of alternatives to Crockford's:

- *The Clergy List . . . .* (C. Cox, 1846–99).
- *The Clergy Directory and Parish Guide: an Alphabetical List of the Clergy of the Church of England . . . .* (Thomas Bosworth, 1873–1930). Annual.
- *Church Directory and Almanac . . . .* (James Nisbet & Co., 1901–47).

High church clergymen of the early twentieth century were listed and 'outed' in:

- *The Ritualistic Clergy List: a guide for patrons & others to certain of the clergy of the Church of England, being a list of over 9,000 clergy men who are helping the Romeward movement in the national church . . . .* (4th ed. Church Association, 1908).

For clergy and their relatives who lost their lives during the First World War, see:

- Ussher, Richard. *Roll of the Sons & Daughters of the Anglican Church Clergy throughout the world, and of the naval & military chaplains of the same, who gave their lives in the Great War 1914-1918.* (English Crafts & Monumental Society, [1925?]).

A number of similar biographical works are listed in:

- Raymond, Stuart A. *Occupational Sources for Genealogists.* (2nd ed. Federation of Family History Societies, 1996).

There are also a number of biographical dictionaries of hymn writers, many of whom were clergy:

- Hayden, Andrew J., and Newton, Robert F. *British Hymn-writers and Composers: a checklist, giving their dates and places of birth and death.* (Hymn Society of Great Britain and Ireland, 1977).
- Thomson, Ronald W. *Who's Who of Hymn Writers.* (Epworth Press, 1967).

Most composers were probably not clergy, but it is worth mentioning:

- Humphreys, Maggie, and Evans, Robert. *Dictionary of Composers for the Church in Great Britain and Ireland.* (Mansell Publishing, 1997).

For published lists of clergy from specific dioceses, see the county volumes of the present author's *British Genealogical Library Guides*. Diocesan calendars (see above, p.137), have regularly listed clergy since the nineteenth century.

There are many more general biographical dictionaries which include clergy. Over 16,000 such dictionaries are listed by:

- Slocum, R.B. *Biographical Dictionaries and Related Works: an International Bibliography.* (2nd ed. Gale Research 1986).

This is indexed in:

- *Biography and Genealogy Master Index: a Consolidated Index to more than 3,200,000 Biographical Sketches in over 350 Current and Retrospective Biographical Dictionaries.* (8 vols. Gale, 1980). Supplements 1981–5, 1986–90, and annually from 1991.

Many of those who held senior office in the Church are included in:

- Oxford Dictionary of National Biography
  www.oxforddnb.com
  This is frequently available free via public library websites. Many libraries also hold the sixty volumes of the printed version.

Biographies
There are numerous biographies and autobiographies of clergy. These can be identified through the catalogues of research libraries such as the British Library. Many can be identified in:

- *Biography Index: a Cumulative Index to Biographical Material in Books and Magazines.* (H.W. Wilson, 1946–).
- *Bibliography of Biography 1970-1984.* (40 fiche + binder. British Library, 1985).

For other relevant bibliographies, see:

- Raymond, Stuart A. *English Genealogy: a Bibliography.* (3rd ed. Federation of Family History Societies, 1996).

Letters and Papers
The papers of over 700 churchmen, from various denominations, are listed in:

- *Papers of British Churchmen, 1780-1940.* (Guides to sources for British history based on the National Archives Register 6. H.M.S.O., 1987).

This listing represents the tip of the iceberg. Many others have been deposited in record offices and libraries, and can be identified by using the union catalogues listed above, pp.53–4.

J. ARMED FORCES CHAPLAINS
Many clergy served as chaplains in the armed forces. Biographical dictionaries and lists are provided by:

• Kealy, A.G. *Chaplains of the Royal Navy, 1626-1903*. (Portsmouth, 1905?)
• Laurence, Anne. *Parliamentary Army Chaplains, 1642-1651*. Royal Historical Society Studies in History 59. (Boydell Press, 1990).
• Taylor, Gordon. *The Sea Chaplains of the Royal Navy.* (Oxford Illustrated Press, 1978).

K. CHAPLAINS OF ROYAL AND ARISTOCRATIC HOUSEHOLDS
The monarch and noblemen could appoint their own domestic chaplains. Lambeth Palace Library holds registers of noblemen's chaplains from 1660 to 1914. Personnel of the Chapel Royal are listed in:

• Baldwin, D. *The Chapel Royal: Ancient and Modern*. (London, 1990).

L. CLERGYMEN OVERSEAS
From the seventeenth century, many clergymen emigrated and founded churches in the colonies and elsewhere. Episcopal oversight of their activities continued to be exercised by the Bishop of London until after American independence was declared. His licences to clergy to serve overseas are in the London Metropolitan Archives. Licences issued between 1676 and 1723 relate mainly to Europe, Africa, America and the West Indies, but are world-wide in their scope. After 1723, and until the end of the eighteenth century, they are almost all for America and the West Indies. Nineteenth- and twentieth-century licences are almost all for Europe.

Other records of the Bishop of London's colonial activities are held amongst Lambeth Palace Library's Fulham Papers. These include numerous testimonials and other ordination papers, especially after 1748. Together with the papers of the Society for the Propagation of the Gospel (see pp.170–1), these papers provide the basic sources needed for the study of American colonial church history. They are calendared in:

- Manross, William Wilson. *The Fulham Papers in the Lambeth Palace Library: American Colonial Section. Calendar and Indexes.* (Clarendon Press, 1965). These papers have been microfilmed, and are available in some major research libraries as *The Fulham Papers at Lambeth Palace Library.* (20 microfilm reels. World Microfilms, c.1970–8).

The clergy of colonial North America are fully listed in:

- Weis, Frederick Lewis. *The Colonial Clergy and the Colonial Churches of New England.* (Society of the Descendants of the Colonial Clergy, 1936). There are similar volumes covering: the Middle and Southern Colonies; Maryland, Delaware and Georgia; Virginia, North Carolina, and South Carolina; New York, New Jersey and Philadelphia.

For those clergymen ordained by the Bishop of London, Weis does not give the dates of ordination, as the registers were missing when he wrote. These are, however, stated in:

- Bell, James B. 'Anglican Clergy in Colonial America Ordained by the Bishops of London', *Proceedings of the American Antiquarian Society*, 83(1) (1973), pp.103–60.

In the eighteenth century, ministers proceeding to North America received a bounty of £20 to pay for their passage. Recipients of this bounty are listed in:

- Fothergill, Gerald. *A List of Emigrant Ministers to America, 1690-1811.* (Elliot Stock, 1914).

For clergy in Australia, see:

- Project Canterbury: Cable Clerical Index
  http://anglicanhistory.org/aus/cci/

A similar webpage lists clergy in New Zealand and the South Pacific:

- Project Canterbury: The Blain Biographical Directory of Anglican Clergy in the South Pacific
  http://anglicanhistory.org/nz/blain_directory

See also:

- Frappell, R., Frappell, L., Nobbs, R., and Withycombe, R., eds. *Anglicans in the Antipodes. An indexed calendar of the papers and correspondence of the Archbishops of Canterbury, 1788-1961, relating to Australia, New Zealand, and the Pacific.* Bibliographies and Indexes in Religious Studies 50. (Greenwood Press, 1999).

The responsibility for appointing chaplains in India lay with the Hon East India Company from c.1600 until 1858. Thereafter, appointments were made by the India Office. The *India Office Lists* include details of chaplains from 1803. For details of sources held by the British Library, consult:

- British Library: Helps for Researchers: Chaplains and Other Clergymen
  www.bl.uk/reshelp/findhelpregion/asia/india/ indiaofficerecordsfamilyhistory/occupations/chaplainsand otherclergymen/chaplains.html

A modern study of East India Company chaplains is provided by:

- O'Connor, Daniel. *The Chaplains of the East India Company, 1601-1858*. (Continuum, 2012).

FURTHER READING
There are a number of useful books on the history of the clergy. See:

- Heeney, Brian. *A Different Kind of Gentleman: Parish Clergy as Professional Men in early and mid-Victorian England*. (Archon Books, for the Conference on British Studies and Wittenberg University, 1976).
- Jacob, W.M. *The Clerical Profession in the Long Eighteenth Century, 1680-1840*. (Oxford University Press, 2007).
- McClatchey, Diana. *Oxfordshire Clergy 1777-1869: a study of the established church and of the role of its clergy in local society*. (Clarendon Press, 1960).
- O'Day, Rosemary. *The English Clergy: the Emergence and Consolidation of a Profession. 1558-1642*. (Leicester University Press, 1979).
- Pruett, John. *The Parish Clergy under the Later Stuarts: the Leicestershire Experience*. (University of Illinois Press, 1978).
- Russell, Anthony. *The Clerical Profession*. (S.P.C.K., 1984). For the nineteenth and twentieth centuries.

A detailed guide to tracing Anglican clergymen is provided by:

- Towey, Peter. *My Ancestor was an Anglican Clergyman*. (Society of Genealogists Enterprises, 2006).

See also:

- Lambeth Palace Library Research Guide: Biographical Sources for Anglican Clergy
  www.lambethpalacelibrary.org/files/clergy_guide_3.pdf

Two online guides to researching London clergymen could usefully be read by those with interests in other dioceses:

- How Can I Research a London Clergyman?
  **www.open.ac.uk/Arts/building-on-history-project/
  resource-guide/source-guides/Londonclergyman.pdf**
- Sources for tracing Clergy and Church officials
  **www.cityoflondon.gov.uk/things-to-do/london-metro
  politan-archives/visitor-information/Documents/57-
  sources-for-tracing-clergy-and-church-officials.pdf**

Chapter 11

OTHER SOURCES

Previous chapters have described the principal sources likely to provide information about Anglican ancestors. Valuable information may also be found in a wide range of other sources; indeed, many sources which are primarily concerned with other matters may provide useful clues for tracing Anglican ancestors. It is impossible to provide a comprehensive survey of these sources; however, some of the most important are discussed below.

A. CHARLES BOOTH'S INTERVIEWS

Between 1886 and 1903, Charles Booth interviewed 1,800 clergymen for his *Life and Labour of the People*. The majority were Anglicans from the Dioceses of London and Southwark. Most questions concerned the involvement of local churches in society. The interviewer was expected to comment on the character, reliability and, in some cases, appearance of the clergyman in question. The original notebooks, held by the London School of Economics, contain much more information than the published work. They are indexed by:

- Charles Booth Online Archive: Charles Booth and the survey into life and labour in London (1886-1903)
  http://booth.lse.ac.uk

B. DIARIES

Diaries provide invaluable evidence for both family and local historians. Many have been published, and are listed by:

- Havlice, P.P. *And So To Bed: a Bibliography of Diaries published in English*. (Scarecrow Press, 1987).

- Matthews, W. *British Diaries: an annotated bibliography of British Diaries written between 1641 and 1942*. (University of California Press, 1950).

For unpublished nineteenth-century diaries, see:

- Batts, J.S. *British Manuscript Diaries of the 19th century: an annotated listing*. (Centaur Press, 1976).

Many others can be identified in the union catalogues listed above, p.58. Diarists included many parish clergy, whose work is frequently particularly useful for local historians. A number of published clerical diaries have attained the status of classics, and have appeared in many editions; indeed, two of these have had societies created specifically for their study. Publications include (listed by date of compilation):

- Webster, Tom, ed. *The Diary of Samuel Rogers 1634-1638*. (Church of England Record Society 11. 2004).
- Macfarlane, Alan, ed. *The Diary of Ralph Josselin, 1616-1683*. Records of Social and Economic History new series 3. (Oxford University Press for the British Academy, 1976). The diary commences in 1641 (although prefaced by earlier biographical notes), and is also available online at: 'Earls Colne: Records of an English Village 1375–1854' **http://linux02.lib.cam.ac.uk/earlscolne/**
- Hannah, G., ed. *The Deserted Village: the Diary of an Oxfordshire Rector, James Newton, of Nunton Courtenay 1736-86*. (Alan Sutton, 1992).
- Christie, O.F., ed. *The Diary of the Revd. William Jones, 1777-1821, curate and vicar of Broxbourne and the hamlet of Hoddesdon, 1781-1821*. (Brentano's, 1929).
- Wilson, Michael, ed. *The Diary of John Longe, (1765-1834), Vicar of Coddenham*. (Suffolk Record Society, 51. 2008).

- Wells, Roger, ed. *Victorian Village: the Diaries of the Rev. John Coker Egerton, curate and rector of Burwash, East Sussex, 1857-1888*. (Alan Sutton, 1992).
- Plomer, William, ed. *Selections from the Diary of the Rev. Francis Kilvert*. (3 vols. Jonathan Cape, 1938–40). Covers 1870–9. There are various later editions; also, see Grice, Frederick, *Who's Who in Kilvert's Diary*. (Kilvert Society, 1977). The Kilvert Society **www.thekilvertsociety.org.uk** promotes the study of all things Kilvertian.
- Winstanley, R.L., and Jameson, P., eds. *The Diary of James Woodforde*. (17 vols. Parson Woodforde Society, 1977–2007). Covers the period 1758–1802. The fullest edition, but there are many others. See, for example, Woodforde, James. *The Diary of a Country Parson. 1758-1802*, ed. J. Beresford. (Oxford University Press, 1978). Other editions are listed on The Parson Woodforde Society's website **www.parsonwoodforde.org.uk/index.htm**

C. COMMONWEALTH AND INTERREGNUM RECORDS, 1642–1660

The Civil War had a radical effect on the administration of the Church. Its governing hierarchy was abolished, and replaced by various Parliamentary committees and trustees. Reference has already been made to those records relating to clergy (see above, pp.186–7)

In 1646, and again in 1649, Parliament ordered the sale of all lands belonging to bishops, deans and chapters. Surveys of these lands, listing tenants, were undertaken. In the event, not all of the land was sold; some was leased. Many records are held by Lambeth Palace Library, and listed in:

- Houston, Jane. *Catalogue of Ecclesiastical Records of the Commonwealth 1643-1660 in the Lambeth Palace Library*. (Gregg International, 1968).

Relevant records are also held amongst diocesan archives, by the

Parliamentary Archives, and in the British Library. For an example of a Parliamentary survey in print, see:

• Kirby, D.A., ed. *Parliamentary Surveys of the Bishopric of Durham*. (2 vols. Surtees Society 183 & 185. 1968–72).

D. THE COMPTON CENSUS 1676
This census, instigated by the Bishop of London, counted the number of inhabitants in each parish, together with the numbers of Nonconformists and Roman Catholics. A full transcription of the principal manuscripts is provided by:

• Whiteman, Anne, ed. *The Compton Census of 1676: a Critical Edition*. Records of social and economic history new series 10. (Oxford University Press for the British Academy, 1986).

E. THE ECCLESIASTICAL CENSUS 1851
On Sunday, 30 March 1851, the Home Office took a census of religion. It identified the places of worship of every denomination, giving their dates of erection and the names of their ministers. It also counted the numbers of attendees at morning and evening worship, and the number of children attending Sunday School. The records are now in The National Archives, class HO 129, and have been digitized for download. Returns for a number of counties have been published, and are listed by:

• Field, Clive Douglas. 'The 1851 Religious Census of Great Britain: A Bibliographical Guide for Local and Regional Historians', *Local Historian* Vol. 27 (1997), pp. 194–217. Updated at **www.brin.ac.uk/commentary/drs/appendix2**

A more recent edition, with a valuable introduction, is provided by:

• Munden, Alan, ed. *The Religious Census of Bristol and Gloucestershire 1851*. Gloucestershire Record Series 29. (Bristol & Gloucestershire Archaeological Society, 2015).

The interpretation of census data is problematic, since there is no way of telling how many attended both morning and evening services, or how many attended two services on the same day. Also, some ministers refused to provide the information required. Anglicans were horrified to discover that about half of those who attended worship were Nonconformists, and that well over half of the population did not attend church at all. All that can be said is that a minimum of 35 per cent of the population attended church on Census Sunday.[1]

The returns provide a rich mine of data for studying the history of all denominations. A detailed guide for researchers (although its references to microfilm are outdated) is provided by:

• Family & Community Historical Research Society: Bums on Pews: the 1851 Religious Census
  https://web.archive.org/web/*/www.fachrs.com/pages/ members/papers/b_o_p.htm

F. GLYNNE'S CHURCH NOTES
Sir Stephen Glynne was an antiquary who made architectural notes on 5,150 churches in many counties. These include a few notes on inscriptions. His notebooks are now housed in Flintshire Record Office. Many of them have been published; publications are listed by Wikipedia **https://en.wikipedia.org/wiki/Sir_Stephen_Glynne_9th _Baronet**. See, for example:

• Hopkinson, Aileen, Hopkinson, Vincent, and Bateman, Wendy, eds. *The Derbyshire Church Notes of Sir Stephen Glynne, 1825-1873.* (Derbyshire Record Society, 32. 2004).

G. NEWSPAPERS
Newspapers frequently reported on parish events, vestry decisions, and clergymen going about their calling. Many have been digitized, and are available, pay per view (but free on some public library sites) at:

- British Newspaper Archive
  www.britishnewspaperarchive.co.uk

Numerous other newspapers are available in the:

- British Library's Newspaper collection
  **http://www.bl.uk/reshelp/findhelprestype/news/
  blnewscoll/**
  This collection includes many denominational newspapers,
  which are frequently particularly useful for obituaries. Many of
  these newspapers were published, but the two most important
  current weeklies are
- *The Church Times*. 1863– . Its archive is available at
  www.churchtimes.co.uk/archive
- *Church of England Newspaper*. 1828– .

Two older titles, now ceased publication, are also worth mentioning:

- *The Ecclesiastical Gazette*. (monthly). July 1838–May 1900.
- *The Guardian: the Church Newspaper* (weekly). 1846–1951.

For a detailed listing of other religious newspapers and journals,
consult:

- Altholz, Josef. *The Religious Press in Britain, 1760-1900*.
  (Greenwood Press, 1998).

Local newspapers are particularly important. Some are included in
the database mentioned above, but many others are available on
microfilm. For a full listing, with details of availability, see:

- Gibson, Jeremy, Langston, Brett, and Smith, Brenda W. *Local
  Newspapers 1750-1920: England and Wales, Channel Islands, Isle of
  Man: a select location list*. (3rd ed. Family History Partnership,
  2011).

H. *NOTITIA PAROCHIALIS*

In 1705, just after the Foundation of Queen Anne's Bounty, a private survey of the Church was initiated. Parish clergy were asked to answer the following questions:

1. Are the Tythes, or any part of them impropriated, and for whom?
2. What part of the Tythes is your Church or Chapel endowed with?
3. What Augmentation or other Benefaction has your Benefice had, when and by whom?
4. If your Church or Chapel was founded since the Reformation when and by whom?
5. What Union or Dismemb'ring (if any) has been made of your Church, and by whom?
6. What Library is settled or sett'ling in your Parish and by whom?
7. If the Yearly Value of your Rectory, Vicarage or Chapelry be under 30 li. how much?
8. To whom does the Advowson, Collation or Donation of your Benefice belong?
9. If it be conominal with any other Place, what is the Note of Distinction?
10. If it be a Benefice that is not taken notice of in the *Valor Beneficiorum*, pray express in what Archdeaconry or Deaconry it is.

Answers were received from 1,576 parishes (out of over 11,000); they are now held in Lambeth Palace Library, mss. 960-5. For the Buckinghamshire returns, see:

• Rouse, E. Clive. 'The *Notitia Parochialis*', *Records of Buckinghamshire* 17(5) (1965), pp.403–5.

I. QUEEN ANNE CHURCHES

When the roof of St Alphage's church in Greenwich collapsed in 1710, it triggered a campaign which led to the creation of the Commission for Building Fifty New Churches. The archives of the Commission include its minutes, numerous, deeds, contracts and a variety of other papers. They are listed in:

• Bill, E.G.W. *The Queen Anne Churches. A catalogue of the papers in Lambeth Palace Library of the Commission for Building Fifty New Churches in London and Westminster, 1711-1759.* (Mansell, 1979).

For a full transcript of the minute books, which include many names, see:

• Port, M.H. *The Commission for Building Fifty New Churches. The minute books, 1711-1727. A calendar.* (London Record Society, vol. 23, 1986).

J. SCHOOL RECORDS

Mention has already been made of clergy involvement in education (see p.179), and of the schools established by the National Society (see pp.162–5). These were primarily for the lower classes. It is also important to appreciate that many of the most prominent Victorian public schools, which catered for the upper classes, were originally established as Anglican charities and employed numerous clergymen as teachers. Consequently, the elite had an Anglican education. Many registers of public schools, listing both staff and students, have been published. See:

• Jacobs, P.M. *Registers of the Universities, Colleges, and Schools of Great Britain and Ireland: a list.* (Athlone Press, 1966).

An extensive collection of school registers is held by the Society of Genealogists. For its holdings, see:

The pulpit at Woodbastwick in Norfolk.

St Matthew's, Exeter – a good example of a late Victorian church.

- *School, University and College Registers and histories in the Library of the Society of Genealogists.* (2nd ed. Society of Genealogists, 1996).

For a detailed guide to educational records, see:

- Chapman, Colin R. *The Growth of British Education and its Records.* (Lochin Publishing, 1992).

Local historians should also consult:

- Stephens, W.B., and Unwin, R.W. *Materials for the Local and Regional Study of Schooling, 1700-1900.* Archives and the user 7. (British Records Association, 1987).

K. SERMONS

Until the nineteenth century, sermons and religious pamphlets were one of the most important publishing genres. Many clergy published at least a single sermon. Sermons are likely to indicate the theological leanings and ideas of their authors, and may also provide incidental information on local events. Many are held in the British Library, Lambeth Palace Library, and other research libraries.

NOTES

CHAPTER 1: THE HISTORY OF THE CHURCH OF ENGLAND
1. Nicholas Harpsfield, Marian Archdeacon of Canterbury, quoted in Raymond, Stuart A. *Tracing your Ancestors' Parish Records*. (Pen & Sword, 2015), p.61.
2. Yet within four years of her accession no less than 41 per cent of the clergy of the Archdeaconry of Norwich had married; cf. Houlbrooke, Ralph. *Church Courts and the People during the English Reformation, 1520-1570*. (Oxford University Press, 1979), p.183. For married clergy during the Edwardian and Marian periods, see O'Day, Rosemary. *The English Clergy: the Emergence and Consolidation of a Profession, 1558-1624*. (Leicester University Press, 1929), p.29.
3. A biographical dictionary of exiles is provided by Garrett, Christina Hallowell. *Marian Exiles: a study in the origins of Elizabethan Puritanism*. (Cambridge University Press, 1938).
4. For the staunch independence of her bishops, and their difficulties with the Queen, see Collinson, Patrick. *The Religion of Protestants: the Church in English Society 1559-1625*. (Clarendon Press, 1982), pp.35–8.
5. John Foxe's *The Acts and Monuments*. (4th ed. 1583). Various editions of this work are available online; most are listed at **http://onlinebooks. library.upenn.edu**.
6. Although the term did not become common until nineteenth-century Tractarians adopted its use; cf. Davies, Julian. *The Caroline Captivity of the Church: Charles I and the Remoulding of Anglicanism*. (Clarendon Press, 1992), pp.5–7.
7. Collinson, *The Religion of Protestants*, op cit, p.82.
8. Printed in part by Kenyon, J.P., ed. *The Stuart Constitution: documents and commentary*. (Cambridge University Press, 1966), pp.461–2.
9. For these records, see Raymond, Stuart A. *Tracing Your Ancestors in County Records: a Guide for Family and Local Historians*. (Pen & Sword, 2016), pp.111–20; Raymond, Stuart A. *Tracing Your Nonconformist Ancestors: a Guide for Family and Local Historians*. (Pen & Sword, 2017), pp.48–9.
10. For records of Quaker Sufferings, see Raymond, *Tracing Your Nonconformist Ancestors*, op cit, pp.131–3. Detailed accounts of sufferings

are printed in Besse, Joseph. *Sufferings of Early Quakers in Yorkshire, 1652-1690: facsimile of part of the 1753 edition*, with new introduction by Michael Gandy. (Sessions Book Trust, c1998). Further volumes cover other parts of Britain.

11. Tarver, Anne. *Church Court Records: an Introduction for Family and Local Historians*. (Phillimore, 1995), p.35.

12. If indeed it had been absent; few churchwardens' accounts record the purchase of its replacement, Parliament's *Directory*, and it is evident that it continued to be used – perhaps widely.

13. Jacob, W.M. *Lay People and Religion in the Early Eighteenth Century*. (Cambridge University Press, 1996), p.55.

14. That is, the holding of more than one benefice.

15. On the non-jurors, see: The Theologies of the Nonjurors: A Historiographical Essay / Robert D. Cornwall **www.cromohs.unifi.it/seminari/cornwall_nonjuror.html**. This is now available through the Internet Archive **https://archive.org**. A listing of both clerical and non-clerical non-jurors is printed in Overton, J.H. *The Non-Jurors: their Lives, Principles, and Writings*. (Smith, Elder & Co., 1902), pp.467–96.

16. Cited by Sykes, Norman. *From Sheldon to Secker: Aspects of English Church History, 1660-1768*. (Cambridge University Press, 1959), p.200.

17. Walsh, John, et al. *The Church of England c.1689-c.1833*. (Cambridge University Press, 1993), p.13.

18. Gregory, Jeremy. *Restoration, Reformation, and Reform, 1660-1828: Archbishops of Canterbury and their Diocese*. (Clarendon Press, 2000), pp.16, 153, and 177.

19. For their numbers in 1676, see Whiteman, Anne, ed. *The Compton Census of 1676: a critical edition*. Records of social and economic history new series 10. (Oxford University Press for the British Academy, 1986).

20. Gregory, *Restoration, Reformation, and Reform*, op cit, p.18.

21. Information regarding recusants could nevertheless be gathered by the church courts and passed on to Quarter Sessions, whose penal powers were much greater.

22. Spaeth, Donald A. *The Church in an Age of Danger: parsons and parishioners, 1660-1740*. (Cambridge University Press, 2000), p.63.

23. Virgin, Peter. *The Church in an Age of Negligence: ecclesiastical structure and problems of church reform, 1700-1840*. (James Clarke & Co., 1989), p.144.

24. Ibid., pp.163–4.

25. Paragraph, Peter. *The Methodist and mimick: a tale, in Hudibrastick verse*.

(1766), quoted by Warne, Arthur. *Church and Society in Eighteenth-Century Devon.* (David & Charles, 1969), p.111.

26. For the Clapham Sect, see Tomkins, Stephen Michael. *The Clapham Sect: How Wilberforce's circle changed Britain.* (Lion Hudson, 2010); Howse, Ernest Marshall. *Saints in Politics: "Clapham Sect" and the Growth of Freedom.* (Allen & Unwin, 1971).

27. For these societies, see Chapter 9.

28. For the Oxford Movement, see Nockles, Peter B. *The Oxford Movement in Context: Anglican High Churchmanship 1760-1857.* (Cambridge University Press, 1994).

29. Virgin, *The Church in an Age of Negligence*, op cit, pp.5 and 34.

30. Port, M. H. *600 New Churches: the Church Building Commission 1818-1856.* (Spire Books, 2006), p.22.

31. Knight, Frances. *The Nineteenth Century Church and English Society.* (Cambridge University Press, 1995), p.64.

32. Virgin, *The Church in an Age of Negligence*, op cit, p.158; Burns, Arthur. *The Diocesan Revival in the Church of England c.1800-1870.* (Clarendon Press, 1999), pp.204–5.

33. For Nonconformity, see Raymond, *Tracing Your Nonconformist Ancestors*, op cit.

34. For an introduction to the 1851 religious census, see Coleman, B.I. *The Church of England in the Mid-Nineteenth Century: a Social Geography.* (Historical Association, 1980).

35. McLeod, Hugh. *Religion and Society in England 1850-1914.* (Macmillan Press, 1996), p.11.

36. Virgin, *The Church in an Age of Negligence*, op cit, pp.5–6.

37. Rosman, Doreen. *The Evolution of the English Churches, 1500-2000.* (Cambridge University Press, 2003), p.208.

38. Chadwick, Owen. *The Victorian Church, part II.* (Adam & Charles Black, 1970), pp.221–3.

39. For these statistics, see Brooks, Chris, and Saint, Andrew, eds. *The Victorian Church: Architecture and Society.* (Manchester University Press, 1995), pp.9–10. Cooper, Trevor, and Brown, Sarah, eds. *Pews, Benches & Chairs: church seating in English parish churches from the fourteenth century to the present.* (Ecclesiological Society, 2011), p.43.

40. Edwards, David L. *Christian England.* (Combined ed. Fount Paperbacks, 1989), v.3, p.206.

41. Wilson, Michael, ed. *The Diary of John Longe, (1765-1834), Vicar of Coddenham.* Suffolk Record Society, 51. (2008), p.xxv. Hymn singing is

discussed by Wolffe, J. 'Praise to the Holiest in the Height: Hymns and Church Music', in Wolffe, John, ed. *Religion in Victorian Britain, vol.5. Culture and Empire*. (Manchester University Press, 1997), pp.58–99.
42. Wolffe, 'Praise to the Holiest in the Height', op cit, p.65.
43. Ibid, p.93.
44. Cox, Jeffrey. *The English Churches in a Secular Society: Lambeth, 1870-1930*. (Oxford University Press, 1982), p.7.
45. For inscriptions in family bibles, see King, Rena. *The Family Bible: a Priceless Heirloom: its history and evolvement with Inscriptions of Family History Events*. (Family History Partnership, 2014).
46. The history of the church during the war is recounted in Wilkinson, Alan. *The Church of England and the First World War*. (S.P.C.K., 1978).
47. Cox, *The English Churches in a Secular Society*, p.120.
48. Rosman, Doreen. *The Evolution of the English Churches, 1500-2000*. (Cambridge University Press, 2003), pp.308–9.
49. Currie, Robert, Gilbert, Alan, and Horsley, Lee. *Churches and Churchgoers: Patterns of Church Growth in the British Isles since 1700*. (Clarendon Press, 1977), p.129. *The Church of England Yearbook 2015*. (Church House Publishing, 2014), p.lxv.
50. Cooper and Brown, eds. *Pews, Benches & Chairs*, op cit, p.53.

CHAPTER 2: THE STRUCTURE OF THE CHURCH OF ENGLAND
1. For Quarter Sessions records, see Raymond, *Tracing Your Ancestors in County Records*, op cit.
2. Chapman, Colin. *Sin, Sex, and Probate: Ecclesiastical Courts, Officials, & Records*. (2nd ed., updated, Lochin Publishing, 2009).
3. Gregory, *Restoration, Reformation, and Reform*, op cit, p.35.
4. Burns, Arthur. *The Diocesan Revival in the Church of England, c.1800-1870*. (Clarendon Press, 1999), pp.75–107.
5. For the history of the parish, see Pounds, N.J.G. *A History of the English Parish: the Culture of Religion from Augustine to Victoria*. (Rev. ed., Cambridge University Press, 2004). See also Jones, Anthea. *A Thousand Years of the English Parish: Medieval Patterns and Modern Interpretations*. (Windrush Press, 2000).
6. Chadwick, *The Victorian Church, part II*, op cit, p.169.
7. Brooks, Chris, and Saint, Andrew, eds. *The Victorian Church: Architecture and Society*. (Manchester University Press, 1995), p.3.
8. Virgin, *The Church in an Age of Negligence*, op cit, p.36.
9. Ibid, p.173.

10. Jacob, W.M. *The Clerical Profession in the Long Eighteenth Century 1680-1840*. (Oxford University Press, 2007), p.78.
11. Gregory, *Restoration, Reformation, and Reform*, op cit, p.74.
12. Jacob, *The Clerical Profession*, op cit, p.41.
13. Pruett, John H. *The Parish Clergy under the Later Stuarts: the Leicestershire Experience*. (University of Illinois Press), 1978, p.57.
14. Virgin, *The Church in an Age of Negligence*, op cit, p.189 (note 240).
15. Pruett, *The Parish Clergy under the Later Stuarts*, op cit, pp.36 and 63.
16. Virgin, *The Church in an Age of Negligence*, op cit, p.47.
17. For the calculations in this paragraph, see ibid., pp.73–4, 90, 94, 136 and 192–3.
18. For the study of parsonages, see Tiller, Kate. *Parsonages*. (Shire Publications, 2016).
19. Virgin, *The Church in an Age of Negligence*, op cit, p.195.
20. Ibid., p.200.
21. Gregory, *Restoration, Reformation, and Reform*, op cit, p.75.
22. Virgin, *The Church in an Age of Negligence*, op cit,, pp.81 and 111–12.
23. Ibid, p.132.
24. Mumm, Susan. *Stolen Daughters, Virgin Mothers: Anglican Sisterhoods in Victorian Britain*. (Leicester University Press, 1999), p.127.
25. Gregory, *Restoration, Reformation, and Reform*, op cit, p.89.
26. Virgin, *The Church in an Age of Negligence*, op cit, pp.115–21.
27. Jacob, *The Clerical Profession*, op cit, p.229.
28. Edwards, David L. *Christian England*. (Combined ed. Fount Paperbacks, 1989), vol.3, pp.95 and 101.
29. Virgin, *The Church in an Age of Negligence*, op cit, pp.9–11 and 205.
30. For a detailed discussion of this act, see ibid., pp.222–41.
31. Chadwick, *The Victorian Church, part II*, op cit, pp.167–8.
32. Cited by Edwards, *Christian England*, op cit, vol.3, p.162.
33. Virgin, *The Church in an Age of Negligence*, op cit, pp.136 and 202.
34. McLeod, Hugh. *Religion and Society in England 1850-1914*. (Macmillan Press, 1996), p.14.
35. For the appointment and work of parish officers, see Raymond, Stuart A. *Tracing Your Ancestors' Parish Records: a Guide for Family and Local Historians*. (Pen & Sword, 2014).
36. Jacob, *The Clerical Profession*, op cit, p.186.
37. For the role of the parish clerk, see Ditchfield, P.H. *The Parish Clerk*. (Methuen & Co., 1907). Most disappeared in the late nineteenth century, as the abolition of church rates meant their incomes depended on

voluntary contributions, and innovations such as choirs ended their role in services.

38. McLeod, *Religion and Society in England 1850-1914*, op cit, p.167.

CHAPTER 4: PARISH REGISTERS OF BAPTISMS, MARRIAGES AND BURIALS

1. *Letters and papers, foreign and domestic, of the reign of Henry VIII.* Vol. 13(2) (1893), p.486.
2. Cox, J. Charles. *Parish Registers of England.* (Methuen, 1910), pp.2–3.
3. Foxe, John. *The Acts and Monuments of John Foxe*, ed. Stephen Reed Cattley, Vol. 8. (1839), p.298.
4. Gibson, J.S.W., ed. *Baptism and Burial Registers for Banbury, Oxfordshire.* (Banbury Historical Society 7. 1965).
5. Bray, Gerald, ed. *The Anglican Canons 1529-1947.* (Church of England Record Society 6. 1998), p.361.
6. Waters, R.E. Chester. *Parish Registers in England.* (Rev. ed. Longmans Green & Co., 1882; reprinted Family History Society of Cheshire, 1999), p.10.
7. Hobbs, Steve, ed. *Gleanings from Wiltshire Parish Registers.* (Wiltshire Record Society 63. 2010).
8. Firth, C.H., and Rait, R.S., eds. *Acts and Ordinances of the Interregnum, 1642-1660.* (HMSO, 1910), vol. 2, pp.715–18.
9. Raymond, Stuart A. *Parish Registers: a History and Guide.* (Family History Partnership, 2009), p.18.
10. Wiltshire parishes which purchased printed registers in 1783 are listed in Hobbs, *Gleanings from Wiltshire Parish Registers,* op cit, pp.296–7.

CHAPTER 5: OTHER SOURCES OF ANGLICAN BAPTISMS, MARRIAGES AND BURIALS

1. Steel, D.J. *National Index of Parish Registers, Volume 1. Sources of Births, Marriages and Deaths before 1837 (1).* (Society of Genealogists, 1968), p.58.
2. They are discussed in '1822-23: the *annus mirabilis* of genealogy', *Genealogists' Magazine* 21(3) (1983), pp.88–9.
3. Outhwaite, R.B. *The Rise and Fall of the English Ecclesiastical Courts, 1500-1860.* (Cambridge University Press, 2006), p.93.
4. Benton, Tony. *Irregular Marriages in London before 1754.* (2nd ed. Society of Genealogists, 2000), p.20.
5. A few have been published; see Herber, Mark, ed. *Clandestine Marriages in the Chapel and Rules of the Fleet Prison, 1680-1754.* (3 vols. Francis Boutle, 1998–2001).

CHAPTER 6: OTHER PARISH RECORDS

1. Quoted in Knight, *The Nineteenth-century Church and English Society*, op cit, pp.72–3.

2. Raymond, *Tracing Your Ancestors' Parish Records*, op cit, pp.167–8.

3. On the origins of pews, see Barnwell, P.S. 'Seating in the nave of the pre-Reformation parish church', in Cooper, Trevor, and Brown, Sarah, eds. *Pews, Benches & Chairs: Church Seating in English Parish Churches from the Fourteenth Century to the Present*. (Ecclesiological Society, 2011), pp.69–86. This can be read online at **http://ecclsoc. org/resources/publications/**

4. Collinson, *The Religion of Protestants*, op cit, p.188.

5. Knight, *The Nineteenth-century Church and English Society*, op cit, p.67.

6. Hobbs, *Gleanings from Wiltshire Parish Registers*, op cit, p.77.

7. Hanham, Alison, ed. *Churchwardens' Accounts of Ashburton, 1479-1580*. (Devon and Cornwall Record Society new series 15. 1970), p.80.

8. Outhwaite, *The Rise and Fall of the English Ecclesiastical Courts*, op cit, p.88.

9. For a general discussion of sixteenth-century tithe causes, see Houlbrooke, *Church Courts and the People during the English Reformation, 1520-1570*, op cit, pp.117–50.

10. Ibid., p.266.

11. Outhwaite, *The Rise and Fall of the English Ecclesiastical Courts*, op cit, p.87.

12. Houlbrooke, *Church Courts and the People during the English Reformation, 1520-1570*, op cit, p.147.

13. Hobbs, *Gleanings from Wiltshire Parish Registers*, op cit, pp.225–6.

CHAPTER 7: DIOCESAN, CHAPTER AND PROVINCIAL RECORDS

1. Chaucer, Geoffrey. *The Canterbury Tales*. (Rev ed. Penguin Books, 1968), p.311.

2. Sykes, *From Sheldon to Secker*, op cit, p.15.

3. They could also be made when visitations were not in progress.

4. Marchant, Ronald A. *The Church Under the Law: Justice, Administration and Discipline in the Diocese of York 1560–1640*. (Cambridge University Press, 1969), pp.140 and 198–9.

5. Outhwaite, *The Rise and Fall of the English Ecclesiastical Courts*, op cit, p.81.

6. Ibid., p.96.

7. Pruett, *The Parish Clergy under the Later Stuarts*, op cit, pp.119–20.

8. For the decree (in Latin), see Stubbs, William, ed. *Select charters and other illustrations of English Constitutional History from the earliest times to the reign of Edward the First*. (9th ed. Clarendon Press, 1913), pp.99–100.

9. Jacob, *Lay People and Religion in the Early Eighteenth Century*, op cit, p.142.

10. For Quarter Sessions records, and Justices of the Peace, see Raymond, *Tracing Your Ancestors in County Records*, op cit.

11. Ingram, Martin. *Church Courts, Sex and Marriage in England, 1570-1640*. (Cambridge University Press, 1987), p.372.

12. Outhwaite, *The Rise and Fall of the English Ecclesiastical Courts*, op cit, p.84.

13. For office and instance causes, see below.

14. Marchant, *The Church Under the Law*, op cit, pp.30–1 and 182.

15. On the role of the ecclesiastical courts in the enforcement of the Reformation, see Houlbrooke, *Church Courts and the People during the English Reformation*, op cit, pp.242–60.

16. Outhwaite, *The Rise and Fall of the English Ecclesiastical Courts*, op cit, p.83.

17. Ibid., p.64.

18. Ibid., p.98.

19. Morgan, Gwenda, and Rushton, Peter, eds. *The Justicing Notebook (1750-64) of Edmund Tew, rector of Boldon*. (Surtees Society 205. 2000).

20. Ibid., p.40.

21. On excommunication, see Emmison, F.G. *Elizabethan Life: Morals & the Church Courts*. (Essex County Council, 1973), pp.300–7.

22. Jacob, *Lay People and Religion in the Early Eighteenth Century*, op cit, p.150.

23. Quoted by Collinson, *The Religion of Protestants*, op cit, p.56.

24. For a detailed study of these, see Logan, F.D. *Excommunication and the Secular Arm in Medieval England: a study in Legal Procedure from the Thirteenth to the Sixteenth Centuries*. (Toronto: Pontifical Institute of Medieval Studies, 1968). See also Fowler, R.C. 'Secular aid for excommunication', *Transactions of the Royal Historical Society* 8 (1914), pp.113–17.

25. Ingram, *Church Courts, Sex and Marriage in England*, op cit, p.355.

26. See Houlbrooke, *Church Courts and the People during the English Reformation*, op cit, pp.173–213 for a discussion of cases brought against clergy.

27. For benefit of clergy, see Raymond, *Tracing Your Ancestors in County Records*, op cit, pp.156–7.

28. Tarver, Anne. *Church Court Records: An Introduction for Family and Local Historians*. (Phillimore, 1995), p.23.

29. For clergy licences, see Chapter 10.

30. Many Essex examples drawn from licensing documentation are printed in Emmison, *Elizabethan Life: Morals & the Church Courts*, op cit, pp.315–20.

31. Quoted by Mortimer, Ian. 'Diocesan Licensing and Medical Practitioners in South-West England, 1660–1780', *Medical History* 48(1) (2004), pp.49–68. **www.ncbi.nlm.nih.gov/pmc/articles/PMC546295**

32. Much of what follows is based on Chapter 1 of Evenden, Doreen. *The Midwives of Seventeenth-Century London*. (Cambridge University Press, 2000).

33. Cited by Houlbrooke, *Church Courts and the People during the English Reformation*, op cit, p.77.

34. Emmison, *Elizabethan Life: Morals & the Church Courts*, op cit, p.315.

35. The following paragraphs are based on Burns, Arthur. *The Diocesan Revival in the Church of England, c.1800-1870*. (Clarendon Press, 1999), pp.111–14.

36. For a detailed guide to Protestation returns, see Gibson, Jeremy, and Dell, Alan. *The Protestation Returns 1641-42 and Other Contemporary Listings*. (Federation of Family History Societies, 1995. 2004 reprint). The background to oaths of loyalty is discussed in Vallance, E. *Revolutionary England and the National Covenant: State Oaths, Protestantism and the Political Nation, 1553-1682*. (Boydell Press, 2005).

37. For its history, see Usher, Roland G. *The Rise and Fall of the High Commission*. (Clarendon Press, 1913).

38. See ibid., pp.367–71 for a list of surviving records.

39. For these, see 'How to look for Royal grants in letters patent and charters from 1199' **www.nationalarchives.gov.uk/help-with-your-research/research-guides/royal-grants-letters-patent-charters-from-1199**

CHAPTER 8: PROBATE RECORDS

1. Various other minor exclusions are discussed in Cox, Nancy, and Cox, Jeff. 'Probate inventories: the legal background', *Local Historian* 16 (1984), pp.133–45 and 217–27.

2. Kitching, Christopher. 'Probate during the English Civil War and Interregnum', *Journal of the Society of Archivists*, 5 (1976), pp.283–93 and 346–56.

3. Outhwaite, *The Rise and Fall of the English Ecclesiastical Courts*, op cit, p.97.

4. They are edited in Wyatt, Peter, ed. *The Uffculme Wills and Inventories, 16th to 18th centuries*. (Devon & Cornwall Record Society new series 40. 1997).

CHAPTER 9: ANGLICAN CHARITIES, MISSIONS AND RELIGIOUS ORDERS: THEIR STAFF AND THEIR BENEFICIARIES

1. Cox, *The English Churches in Secular Society*, op cit, pp.58–9.

2. Ibid., p.67. The Society's history is recounted in Lewis, Jane. *The Voluntary Sector, The State and Social Work In Britain: the Charity Organisation Society/Family Welfare Association since 1869*. (Edward Elgar, 1995).

3. For a guide to apprenticeship records, see Raymond, Stuart A. *My Ancestor was an Apprentice: How Can I Find Out More About Him?* (Society of Genealogists, 2010).

4. For a general discussion of nineteenth-century national and diocesan associations linked with the Church of England, see Burns, Arthur. *The Diocesan Revival in the Church of England, c.1800-1870*. (Clarendon Press, 1999), pp.114–30.

5. Knight, *The Nineteenth-Century Church and English Society*, op cit, p.125.

6. Ibid.

7. Ibid., p.66.

8. Chadwick, *The Victorian Church, part II*, op cit, pp.173–4.

9. See also Stephens, W.B., and Unwin, R.W. *Materials for the Local and Regional Study of Schooling 1700-1900*. Archives &the User 7. (British Records Association, 1987), pp.25–7.

10. New style dating.

11. For S.P.C.K. archives relating to education, see Stephens and Unwin, *Materials for the Local and Regional Study of Schooling 1700-1900,* op cit, pp.40–3. See also Tate, W.E. 'S.P.C.K. archives with special reference to their value for the history of education', *Archives* 3(18) (1957), pp.105–25.

12. Thomas, T. 'Foreign Missions and Missionaries in Victorian Britain', in Wolffe, John, ed. *Religion in Victorian Britain, vol.5. Culture and Empire.* (Manchester University Press, 1997), p.103.

13. McLeod, *Religion and Society in England 1850-1914,* op cit, p.147.

14. Thomas, 'Foreign Missions and Missionaries in Victorian Britain', op cit, p.105.

15. McLeod, *Religion and Society in England 1850-1914,* op cit, p.147.

16. Mumm, Susan. *Stolen Daughters, Virgin Mothers: Anglican Sisterhoods in Victorian Britain.* (Leicester University Press, 1999), pp.3 and 9.

CHAPTER 10: TRACING ANGLICAN CLERGY
1. Knight, *The Nineteenth-Century Church and English Society,* op cit, p.111.
2. Dowland, David A. *Nineteenth-Century Anglican Theological Training: the Redbrick Challenge.* (Clarendon Press, 1997), p.2.
3. Hastings, Adrian. *A History of English Christianity 1920-1990.* (3rd ed. S.C.M. Press, 1991), p.535.
4. College testimonials were frequently printed, and followed a set formula; they were usually regarded as not worth the paper they were printed on; see Knight, *The Nineteenth-Century Church and English Society,* op cit, p.109.
5. O'Day, *The English Clergy: the Emergence and Consolidation of a Profession,* op cit, pp.12 and 15.
6. Virgin, *The Church in an Age of Negligence,* op cit, p.284.
7. Sykes, Norman. *From Sheldon to Secker: Aspects of English Church History 1660-1768.* (Cambridge University Press, 1959), p.12.
8. For a more detailed discussion of resignation bonds, see Virgin, *The Church in an Age of Negligence,* op cit, pp.185–8.
9. Parliamentary paper 1835, XXII, 1053-6.
10. Sykes, *From Sheldon to Secker,* op cit, pp.41–3.

CHAPTER 11: OTHER SOURCES
1. Rosman, Doreen. *The Evolution of the English Churches, 1500-2000.* (Cambridge University Press, 2003), p.207.

PLACE NAME INDEX

Bedfordshire, 75
Berkshire, 184
   Windsor, 48, 141
Bristol Diocese, 22
Buckinghamshire, 55, 203
   Bierton, 48
   Buckingham Archdeaconry, 114
   Princes Risborough, 92
Cambridgeshire
   Wisbech, 40
Cheshire, 30, 55, 125, 138
   Chester, 119
Chester Diocese, 73
Cornwall, 8, 51, 55
   Cornwall Archdeaconry, 51
   Poundstock, 70, 93
   St. Buryan, 7, 72
   St. Endellion, 132
   St. Levan, 3
   Truro, 109
   Week St Mary, 67
Cumberland, 56
   St. Bees, 176
Derbyshire, 102, 114, 201
   Derby Archdeaconry, 22, 114
Devon, 8, 51, 56, 113
   Ashburton, 94, 98
   Ashton, 5
   Barnstaple, 51
   Broadhembury, 65
   Cockington, 48
   Exeter, 132, 206
   Lundy, 48
   Uffculme, 151
   Whimple, 181

Devon, North, 131
Dorset, 22, 56
   Sherborne, 37
Durham
   Boldon, 122
   Durham, 175
Durham Diocese, 73, 141, 200
Ely Diocese, 184
Essex, 56, 80, 131
   Earls Colne, 198
Exeter Diocese, 51, 114, 133
Gloucestershire & Bristol, 200
   Bristol, 22, 71
   Gloucester, 142
   Tormarton, 175, 182
Hampshire, 56, 115
   Lymington, 118
Hertfordshire
   Datchworth, 102
   Hoddesdon, 198
Ireland, 24
   Dublin, 175
Kent, 76
   Canterbury Diocese, 39, 43, 80,
     113, 132, 139
   Greenwich, 204
Kent, North-West, 76
Lancashire, 56, 75
   Liverpool, 22
   Rochdale, 20
   Walton on the Hill, 94
Lancashire, North, 128
Leicestershire, 111, 195
Lichfield Diocese, 114, 127, 137
Lincoln Diocese, 23, 114

Lincolnshire, 56
  Epworth, 42
  Lincoln, 48, 108, 156, 164
  Lincoln Archdeaconry, 80
  Louth, 92
Llandaff Diocese, 114
London, 22, 32, 47, 54, 56, 71, 75,
  86, 94, 96, 129, 135, 138, 154,
  155, 175, 196, 197, 204
  Aldgate. St. Botolph's, 85
  Dukes Place, St James, 85
  Holy Trinity, Minories, 85
  Liberty of the Fleet, 86
  St. Dunstans' in the West, 66
  St. Pauls, 57
London Diocese, 133, 135, 184, 197
Middlesex, 56
  Chelsea, 135
  Lincoln's Inn, 66
  St. Marylebone, 22
  Westminster, 157
  Westminster Abbey, 48, 141, 204
Monmouthshire
  Magor, 4
Norfolk, 56, 100, 134
  Kings Lynn, 117
  Norfolk Archdeaconry, 114
  Norwich Archdeaconry, 114
  Woodbastwick, 205
Northumberland, 184
  Lindisfarne, 1
Norwich Diocese, 116, 183
Nottinghamshire, 116
  Southwell, 141
Oxfordshire, 56, 130, 131, 195
  Banbury, 66, 115
  Church Hanborough, 89
  Dorchester, 115
  Nunton Courtenay, 198
  Thame, 115

Pembrokeshire
  St. Davids, 38
Rutland, 184
Salisbury Diocese, 22, 115, 183
Scotland
  Aberdeen, 175
  Edinburgh, 175
  Glasgow, 175
  Iona, 1
  St. Andrews, 175
Shropshire, 75
  Battlefield, 67
Somerset, 51, 56
  Wells Cathedral, 142
Staffordshire, 75
  Stafford Archdeaconry, 114
Suffolk, 56, 186
  Coddenham, 25, 198
  Suffolk Archdeaconry, 114
Surrey, 56, 83, 115
  Chichester Diocese, 113
  Kingston upon Thames, 96
  Lambeth, 26, 31, 153
  South Lambeth, 166
  Surrey Archdeaconry, 115
  Wimbledon, 95
Sussex, 56
  Burwash, 199
Wales, 24, 54, 151, 166
Warwickshire, 113
  Birmingham, 76
  No Mans Heath, 48
Westmorland, 56
Wiltshire, 51, 56, 67, 76, 104, 113
  Avebury, 69
  Corsham, 98
  Fontmell Magna, 69
  Monkton Farleigh, 10
  Salisbury, 2, 97, 151
  Steeple Ashton, 4

Stourton, 97, 103
Worcestershire, 102
  Worcester Diocese, 115
York Diocese, 84, 102, 115, 130, 140
Yorkshire, 56, 73, 75, 135
  Beverley, 141
  Craven Archdeaconry, 116
  East Riding Archdeaconry, 115
  Leeds, 22, 24, 179
  Mirfield, 177
  Ripon, 141
  Ripon Diocese, 22
  York Archdeaconry, 115
  York Diocese, 130
  Overseas
  Africa, 172, 192

America, 192
America, North, 170, 192, 193, 194
Atlantic Ocean, 12
Australia, 194
China, 171
Europe, 192
Flanders, 6
Geneva, 8, 9, 12
India, 20, 194, 195
Japan, 171
New Zealand, 194
South Pacific, 194
West Indies, 171, 192

PERSONAL INDEX

Anderson, James, 176
Augustine, 1
Baring-Gould, Sabine, 25
Baxter, Richard, 13
Beaford, Thomas, 67
Bickersteth, Bishop, 116
Bilson, Bishop, 124
Butler, Samuel, 114
Calvin, John, 1
Carlisle, Wilson, 47, 157
Chamberlayne, Edward, 43
Charles I, 11, 12, 67
Charles II, 13
Chaucer, Geoffrey, 106, 107
Cranmer, Thomas, 6, 8, 9, 11, 27, 28, 34

Cromwell, Oliver, 186
Cromwell, Thomas, 6, 64, 65, 66
Dade, William, 73, 79
Davenant, Bishop, 183
Downton, Thomas, 133
Drummond, Archbishop, 116
Edward VI, 6, 8, 65, 66
Egerton, John Coker, 199
Elizabeth I, 9, 10, 11, 34, 35, 66, 125, 183
Forrest, Elizabeth, 135
Foxe, John, 11
George I, 15
Glynne, Stephen, 201
Harpsfield, Archdeacon, 113
Head, John, 36

HenryVIII, 5, 6, 34, 64, 172
Hereford, Bishop of, 23
Herring, Archbishop, 115
Hoare Family, 97
Hook, Walter, 24
Hughes, Joseph, 168
James I, 34, 67
James II, 13, 15, 110
Jewell, Bishop, 10
Jones, Mary, 168
Jones, William, 198
Katherine of Aragon, 5
Kilvert, Francis, 199
Laud, Archbishop, 12, 39, 140
Leir, Thomas, 88
Lincoln, Bishop of, 111
Livingstone, David, 172
London, Bishop of, 47, 192, 193, 200
Longe, John, 198
Luther, Martin, 1
Mahun, Noah, 132
Markham, Archbishop, 73
Mary, Queen, 8, 9, 11, 66, 113, 125
More, Hannah, 20
Neale, J.M., 25
Newton, James, 198
Paragraph, Peter, 18

Pearce, John, 133
Pole, Cardinal, 8, 66
Prideaux, Archdeacon, 15
Raikes, Richard, 20
Redman, Bishop, 114
Rithe, Mr, 66, 67
Rogers, Samuel, 198
Rudolf, Edward De Montjoie, 166
Ryder, Thomas, 134
Sancroft, Archbishop, 15
Secker, Archbishop, 36, 113
Sheldon, Archbishop, 180
Simeon, Charles, 39
Sumner, Mary, 162
Tew, Edmund, 122
Tounson, Bishop, 183
Wake, William, 114
Watson, Joshua, 20
Wesley, John, 18, 19
Wilberforce, William, 20, 168
William I, 116
William III, 13, 15, 125
Wolsey, Cardinal, 6, 64
Woodforde, James, 16, 199
Wycliffe, John, 1
York Diocese, 184
York, Archbishop of, 110, 135

SUBJECT INDEX

Absolution, 124
Accounts, Churchwardens. *See* Churchwardens' Accounts
Accounts, Probate. *See* Probate Accounts
Act Books, 112, 122, 124, 126, 131, 133, 139, 140, 141, 148, 180
Act Books, Chapter, 141, 142
Act of Supremacy, 1558, 140
Additional Curates Society, 20, 157, 159
Administration Bonds, 148, 149

Administrators, 144, 149, 150
Adultery. *See* Sexual Offences
Advowsons, 39, 40, 179, 203
Affidavits, 70, 118
Affidavits, Marriage, 81, 83
Agriculture, 18, 40, 44, 100, 147
AIM, 25, 54
Allegations, Marriage, 80, 83, 84, 85
Alternative Service Book, 28
Ancestry (Website), 60, 76
Anglo-Catholics. *See* High Church
Apparitors, 110, 118, 123, 148
Appraisers, 148
Apprenticeship, 133, 145, 155, 160, 165
Archbishops, 34, 35, 36, 107, 180
Archdeacons, 35, 36, 45, 46, 82, 106, 107, 117, 127, 130, 131
Architecture, 31, 53
Archives, 36, 48, 51, 53, 54, 59, 61, 107, 156, 168, 173, 176, 199
Archives Hub, 54
Archives Wales, 54
Aristocracy, 43, 192
Army Chaplains, 190, 192
Association Oath, 1696, 138
Attendance at Church, 23, 26, 27, 34, 46, 110
Audience Courts, 119, 138, 139, 140
Banns, 68, 71, 74, 81, 82, 84, 85
Baptismal Certificates, 86, 87
Baptisms and Births, 17, 28, 33, 37, 40, 64, 68, 70, 71, 73, 74, 75, 77, 78, 79, 90, 104
Baptisms, Adult, 33, 68
Baptisms, Roman Catholic, 134
Baptists, 12, 14, 33, 68

Bastardy, 33, 111, 116, 120, 121, 122, 134
Bastardy Bonds, 111
Bastardy Examinations, 134
Bedfordshire Necessitous Clergy Society, 157
Benefit of Clergy, 125
Bequests, 147
Bible, Authorised Version, 11, 34
Bibles, 5, 6, 26, 93, 168
Bibliographies, 55, 56, 76, 162, 165, 190, 191, 197
Bills of Costs, 127
Biographical Dictionaries, 56, 175, 188, 189, 190, 191, 199
Biographies, Clergy, 191
Bishops, 34, 35, 36, 117, 125, 143, 178, 179, 180, 183, 187, 199
Bishops' Queries, Replies to, 111, 113, 114, 116, 133, 155
Bishops, Suffragan, 35
Bishops' Transcripts, 67, 78, 80, 106, 174
Blue Coat Schools, 154
Bodleian Library, 171, 172
Bonds. *See* Administration Bonds, Allegations, Marriage, and Resignation Bonds
Book of Common Prayer, 7, 9, 13, 14, 27, 28, 46, 96, 120, 183
Books, 54, 55, 59
Borthwick Institute, 53, 115, 116, 130, 141, 177
Boy Scouts, 154
Boyd's Marriage index, 77
Boys Brigade, 158
British and Foreign Bible Society, 168, 169
British Library, 52, 207

British Library Newspaper
    Collection, 202
British Newspaper Archive, 202
British Record Society, 151
Burials and Death, 33, 40, 64, 68,
    70, 71, 74, 75, 80, 90, 93, 104,
    137
Burials in Woollen, 70
Cadbury Research Library, 159,
    169, 176
Calendars, Diocesan. *See* Diocesan
    Calendars
Call books, 108, 115
Calvinists, 8, 9, 12
Cambridge Clergy Training School,
    177
Cambridge University, 175
Cambridge University Library, 157,
    165, 169
Canon Law, 17, 34, 45, 46, 48, 49,
    80, 81, 82, 85, 116, 120, 136
Canons (Clergy), 36, 141, 185, 186
Catalogues, Library, 55, 57, 58
Catalogues, Union, 53, 54, 57, 58
Cathedrals, 13, 22, 36, 39, 53, 107,
    137, 141, 142, 184, 185, 188
Cause Papers, 123, 128, 130, 140,
    141
Cavalier Parliament, 13, 14
Census, Compton. *See* Compton
    Census
Census, Ecclesiastical, 1851, 23,
    200, 201
Chancellors, 36, 107, 117, 140
Chancery, Court of, 100, 124, 136
Chancery, Court of (York), 119, 140
Chapel Royal, 192
Chapelries, 36, 43
Chaplains, 192, 194, 195

Chapters. *See* Deans & Chapters
Charity and Charities, 37, 43, 48,
    94, 111, 137, 145, 146, 147, 153,
    154, 155, 156, 160, 179, 204
Charity Boards, 155
Charity Commission, 155
Charity Organisation Society, 154
Children, 17, 25, 27, 73, 121, 135,
    144, 145, 147, 148, 149, 153, 155,
    159, 160, 166, 167, 200
Children's Society, 167
Choirs, 25, 47
Church Ales, 92
Church Army, 47, 157
Church Assembly, 27, 28, 34
Church Building Commission, 22,
    143
Church Commissioners, 36, 47, 53,
    107, 143, 185
Church Girls Brigade, 158
Church Lads Brigade, 157, 158
Church Missionary Society, 20,
    169, 170
Church of England Children's
    Society, 167
Church of England Council for
    Social Aid, 159
Church of England Mens Society,
    158
Church of England Newspaper, 202
Church of England Protection
    Society, 160
Church of England Record Centre,
    53, 143, 158, 160, 165
Church of England Sunday School
    Institute, 158
Church of England Temperance
    Society, 159
Church Pastoral Aid Society, 159

Church Plans Online, 162

Church Rates. *See* Rates, Church

Church Times, 202

Church Union, 160, 161

Churchings, 17

Churchwardens, 14, 17, 23, 34, 35, 45, 46, 67, 91, 93, 94, 95, 97, 98, 104, 105, 108, 110, 111, 112, 118, 120, 121, 138, 155

Churchwardens' Accounts, 46, 90, 91, 94, 95, 98, 101

Churchwardens' Presentments. *See* Presentments, Churchwardens'

Citations, 110, 118, 123, 126, 128, 150

Citations with Intimation, 121

Civil Registers, 50, 51, 74

Civil Service Evidences of Age, 87

Civil War, 12, 67, 80, 160, 186, 187, 199

Clapham Sect, 20, 168

Clergy of the Church of England Database, 174, 175, 178, 180, 183

Clergy Orphan Corporation, 159, 160

Clergy, Colonial, 192, 193

Clergy, Ejected 1662, 13, 14, 19, 125, 127, 187

Clergy, Married, 9, 40, 125

Clergy, Royalist, 12, 125, 186, 187

Clerical Dynasties, 40, 43

Clerical Taxation. *See* Taxation Clerical

Close Rolls, 185

Collation, 179, 203

College of the Resurrection, 177

Colleges, Theological, 45, 176, 177

Commissaries, 117

Committee for Plundered Ministers, 186

Committee for Scandalous Ministers, 186

Committee for the Approbation of Public Preachers, 186

Common Worship, 28

Communion, 13, 28, 46, 93, 138

Compton Census, 200

Compurgation, 123

Confirmation, 36, 103

Confirmation Registers, 103

Constables, Parish, 17, 46, 91, 94

Convocation, 24, 34, 35, 68, 184

Copac, 58

Cornwall Record Office, 51

Corporation of the Sons of the Clergy, 160

Correspondence. *See* Letters and Papers

Court of Arches, 35, 138, 139

Courts, Archdeaconry, 36, 116, 117, 119, 130, 131, 144, 150, 151

Courts, Consistory, 17, 100, 116, 117, 119, 129, 139, 140, 144, 150, 151

Courts, Ecclesiastical, 13, 14, 17, 33, 35, 36, 85, 97, 100, 102, 107, 110, 111, 112, 116–32, 138–41, 144, 150. *See also* Probate Courts

Crockford's, 189

Cuddesdon College, 176

Cumbria Archive Service, 176

Curates, 20, 24, 42, 44, 157, 159, 160, 178, 179

Curates, Perpetual, 43

Curates' Augmentation Fund, 160

Curates' Licences, 107, 132, 179

Cyndi's List, 60

Dade registers, 73, 79
Deaconesses, 47
Deacons, 177, 180
Deans and Chapters, 36, 112, 141, 142, 143, 185, 199
Death, 1, 3, 27, 145, 146
Debts, 147, 149
Declarations of Indulgence, 1672 and 1687, 13, 110
Deeds. *See* Title Deeds
Defamation, 106, 110, 121, 122, 128, 131, 139
Depositions, 126, 128, 130, 141, 150
Deprivation, 125
Detection Books, 110, 123
Devon & Cornwall Record Society, 76
Devon Heritage Trust, 51
Diaries, 16, 197, 198, 199
Dictionary of National Biography, 56
Digitised Images, 58, 59, 60, 63, 75, 76, 78, 86, 130, 151, 152, 162, 170, 200, 201
Dilapidations, 121, 125
Diocesan Archives, 46, 48, 51, 80, 83, 87, 106–38, 142, 162, 174, 175, 177, 178
Diocesan Calendars, 137
Dioceses, 22, 34, 35, 47, 51, 107
Discipline, Clerical, 21, 34, 116, 129, 140
Discovery Catalogue, 53, 151
Dispensations, 107, 140, 180
Dissenters. *See* Nonconformists
Dissolution of the Monasteries, 6, 39
District Registrars, 74

E 179 Database, 184
East India Company, 194, 195
Easter Books, 102, 103
Easter Offerings, 40, 45, 103, 120
Ecclesiastical Census, 1851. *See* Census, Ecclesiastical, 1851
Ecclesiastical Commission, 22, 36, 143, 184, 185
Ecclesiastical Gazette, 202
Enclosure Movement, 40, 41, 100
Estate Records, 36, 51, 87, 142, 143
Evangelicalism, 18–21, 24, 39, 167, 176
Exchequer, 183
Exchequer Court (York), 140
Excommunicates, 124, 145
Excommunication, 11, 17, 35, 123–5, 127, 128
Executors, 35, 46, 108, 120, 144, 147, 149, 150
Exhibits, 126
Fabric, 31, 46, 93, 95, 110, 111, 121, 130, 142
Faculties, 117, 121, 130, 139, 140
Faculty Office, 35, 84, 133, 139, 140
Family History Library and Centres, 58, 77
Family History Partnership, 54
Family History Societies, 55, 57, 58, 76, 88
Family Search, 58, 76
Farmers, 40, 41, 44
Fasti Ecclesiae Anglicana, 188
Fathers (Clerical), 21
Federation of Family History Societies, 54, 58, 77
Felons, 145
Feoffees for Impropriations, 39
Fifth Monarchy men, 12, 13

Find My Past, 60, 77, 151
Fines, 124, 140
First Fruits and Tenths, 183, 184, 185
Flintshire Record Office, 201
Fornication. *See* Sexual Offences
Foundling Hospital, 154
Freehold, Parsons', 16, 38, 47, 112, 180
Fulham Papers, 193
Funerals, 17, 28, 37, 90, 149
Genealogist (website), 60
General Register Office, 74
General Synod, 35, 53
Genes Reunited, 77
Gentry, 34, 39, 44, 87, 96, 124
Genuki, 60, 76, 81
Girls Friendly Society, 161
Glebe, 38, 40, 41, 45, 47, 112, 179
Glebe Terriers, 101, 103, 106, 112, 113
Godparents, 66, 67, 103
Google, 76
Google Books, 59
Guardian: the Church Newspaper, 202
Guardians, 71, 83, 149
Hackney Phalanx, 20, 22
Handwriting, 61, 62, 123, 128
Hardwicke's Marriage Act. *See* Marriage Act, 1753
Harleian Society, 75
Hathi Trust Digital Library, 59
High Church, 12, 20, 21, 27, 53, 159, 160, 189
High Commission, 140, 141
High Court of Delegates, 141
Highway Surveyors, 46, 91, 94
Household Goods, 148

Hundreds, 142
Hymn Writers, 190
Hymns, 9, 25, 26, 47
Impropriation and Impropriators, 39, 99, 100, 107, 203
Incomes, Clergy, 18, 40, 41, 43, 44, 45, 112, 160, 183, 184, 185
Incorporated Church Building Society, 20, 22, 98, 161, 162
Incumbents' Visiting Books, 103, 104
Independents, 12, 14
Index Library, 151
Indexes, 54, 55, 58, 60, 63, 76, 77, 78, 80
Indexes, Marriage. *See* Marriage Indexes
Indexes, Wills, 151, 152
India Office lists, 194
Industrialization, 18, 21, 73
Inheritance, 64, 74, 86, 145
Injunctions, 64, 65, 66, 113, 136
Inns of Court, 48
Instance Business, 117, 120, 121, 122
Institutions (Clergy), 174, 178, 180, 186
International Genealogical Index, 77
Internet, 50, 51, 55, 58, 59, 60, 61, 63, 75, 76, 81, 88, 90, 151, 175, 191
Internet Archive, 59
Interregnum, 12, 18, 68, 80, 81, 116, 125, 150, 160, 186, 187, 199
Interrogatories, 126, 150
Jews, 71, 86
Joiner Marriage Index, 77
Josselin, Ralph, 198

Justices of the Peace, 37, 43, 44, 68, 100, 111, 116, 120, 121, 122, 127
Kelham Hall, 177
Kett's Rebellion, 100
Kilvert Society, 199
Kings Bench, 136
King's Evil, 94
Laity, 16, 17, 27, 46, 47, 120, 123, 154, 184
Laity, House of, 34, 35
Lambeth Degrees, 175
Lambeth Palace Library, 52, 53, 84, 134, 139, 143, 157, 158, 159, 160, 161, 162, 165, 166, 171, 173, 175, 180, 186, 192, 193, 195, 199, 203, 204, 207
Latin, 61, 62, 149
Latter Day Saints, 58, 77
Laudians, 12
Letters and Papers, 51, 101, 104, 155, 157, 161, 165, 166, 169, 191, 192, 194
Letters Dimissory, 177
Letters Patent, 141
Libel (accusation), 122, 126
Liber cleri, 109
Liberation Society, 24
Libraries, 50, 51, 54, 57, 58, 59, 61, 104, 191, 192, 193, 207
Liturgy, 9, 14, 25, 27, 28, 53, 136
Local History Societies, 59
Lollardy, 1
London College of Divinity, 176, 177
London Metropolitan Archives, 76, 160, 192
London School of Economics, 161, 197

Loyalty Oaths. See Oaths, Loyalty
Lunatics, 145
Manors, 142
Marriage Act, 1753, 71, 83, 86
Marriage Act, 1824, 81
Marriage Indexes, 77
Marriage Licences, 35, 48, 80, 82, 83, 84, 85, 87, 106, 140, 142
Marriage Registers, 61, 71, 73, 74, 75, 81, 82
Marriages, 17, 28, 33, 37, 40, 64, 66, 68, 70, 71, 74, 75, 78, 79, 81, 82, 90, 104, 121, 139
Marriages, Clandestine, 71, 85, 86, 124
Medway Archives, 76
Methodism, 18, 19, 23, 26, 73
Midwives, 134, 135
Midwives' Licences, 107, 120, 131, 134
Missionaries, 167, 168, 169, 170–1
Missionary Societies, 48, 153, 167, 168, 169, 170, 171, 172
Monumental Inscriptions, 87, 90
Morals, 33, 35, 46, 111, 116, 120, 129, 131, 136, 139
Mothers' Union, 105, 162
Muggletonians, 12
Mundus, 168
Music, 24, 26
National Archives, 52, 53, 61, 174, 191
ADM 6, 13 and 107, 87
C 214, 137
C 224, 138
C 54, 185
C 66, 180
C207/1-12 and 23, 125
C85, 125

CHES 38/25/4-6, 125
CHES 4, 138
DEL, 141
E 179, 184
E 196, 138
E 33144 and 347, 183, 184
HO 129, 200
IR 18 and 29–30, 101
KB 22, 138
PROB 11, 151
QAB 1, 183
RG 7, 86
SP 22, 186
WO 32/8903-20, 87
WO 42, 87
National Burial Index, 77
National Index of Parish Registers,
    75, 78, 81
National Library of Wales, 151
National Society, 20, 53, 158, 162,
    164, 165, 204
Newspapers, 201, 202
Nonconformists, 14, 16, 17, 23, 24,
    34, 35, 71, 73, 82, 92, 99, 110,
    111, 127, 138, 157, 158, 200, 201
Non-jurors, 125, 188
Non-Residence, 37, 42–4, 125, 140
North Devon Record Office, 51
Northern Province, 53, 84, 115,
    129, 134, 136, 140, 144
Notitia Parochialis, 203
Nuns, 47
Oaths, 118, 136
Oaths, Clergy, 15, 108, 183
Oaths, Executors, 150
Oaths, Loyalty, 136, 137, 138
Oaths, Schoolmasters, 136
OCLC World Cat, 58
Office Business, 120, 121, 122

Official (Judge), 107, 117
Official Principal, 140
Open Library, 59
Ordinands, 16, 43, 45, 175, 176,
    177, 178, 180, 187
Ordination, 16, 36, 87, 174, 175,
    178, 179, 183, 193
Ordination Papers, 87, 178, 193
Ordination, Women, 47
Ordinations, 45, 137, 174, 178, 180,
    187
Organs and Organists, 24, 25, 45,
    92, 93, 95
Overseers, 37, 46, 91, 94, 155
*Oxford Dictionary of National
    Biography*, 191
Oxford Diocesan Church Building
    Society, 157
Oxford Movement, 20, 21, 24, 25
Oxford University, 175
Palaeography. *See* Handwriting
Pallot's Index, 77
Parish Chests and Records, 51, 70,
    81, 83, 91, 93, 101, 102, 103, 104,
    105, 112, 145, 146, 155, 157, 158,
    168, 185
Parish Clerks, 46, 47, 95, 132
Parish Constables. *See* Constables,
    Parish
Parish Magazines, 90, 104
Parish Register Society, 76
Parish Register Transcription
    Society, 76
Parish Registers, 48, 51, 60, 61, 63,
    64-81, 90, 101, 126, 135, 142,
    174
Parish Registers, Interregnum, 68
Parishes, 17, 35–8, 47, 48, 51, 91,
    95, 137, 142, 143, 179, 185, 203

Parliamentary Surveys. *See* Surveys, Parliamentary

Parsonages, 41, 43, 112, 121

Parsons' Freehold. *See* Freehold, Parsons'

Pastoral Measure, 1968, 47

Patent Rolls, 180

Patrons, 34, 39, 174, 179, 181, 189

Paupers, 73, 94, 97

Peculiars, 36, 47, 48, 80, 82, 85, 112, 115, 119, 142, 144, 151

Peculiars, Royal, 141

Pen & Sword, 54

Penance, 17, 35, 112, 123, 124, 125, 127

Pensions, Clergy, 47

Peterloo, 44

Pew Rents, 161

Pews, 96, 98, 99, 120, 121

Phillimore Parish Registers, 75, 76

Photographs, 53, 90, 161

Pilgrim Fathers, 12

Pilgrimage of Grace, 6, 64

Plenary Proceedings, 122, 126

Pluralism, 15, 37, 41, 44, 47, 99, 140, 180

Pluralities Acts, 1838 and 1850, 18, 44, 179

Police Court Missionaries, 159

Poll Taxes, 184

Poor Law, 46, 91

Prayer Book. *See Book of Common Prayer*

Preachers, 7, 43, 138, 186

Preachers' Licences, 107, 132

Prerogative Court of Canterbury, 35, 139, 144, 150, 151, 152

Prerogative Court of York, 35, 140, 144, 150

Presbyterianism, 12, 14

Presentations, 39, 142, 180, 181, 186

Presentments, Churchwardens', 14, 17, 108-111, 113-115, 120, 121, 123, 128, 132, 148, 150

Probate Accounts, 149

Probate Causes, 121, 122, 127, 128, 150

Probate Court (Interregnum), 150

Probate Courts, 35, 48, 119, 129, 139–42, 144, 146-52

Probate Inventories, 147, 148, 149

Probate Records, 63, 144–52, 174, *See* also Administration Bonds, Probate Accounts, Probate Inventories, and Wills

Probation Service, 159

Proctors, 118, 123, 126

Protestation Oath, 1641/2, 138

Provinces, 35, 47, 133, 134, 138, 140

Psalms, 24, 25, 47

Purgatory, 3

Puritans, 12, 13, 23, 24, 33, 39, 92, 129, 140, 188

Pusey House, 53, 173

Quakers, 12, 14, 33, 68, 71, 86, 99

Quarter Sessions, 14, 17, 33, 51, 94, 116, 120–2, 125, 136, 138

Queen Anne Churches, 204

Queen Anne's Bounty, 143, 183, 185, 203

Ranters, 12, 13

Rates, Church, 23, 24, 45, 46, 91, 92, 95, 120

Recognizances, 122

Record Offices, 50–3, 59, 75, 81, 101, 104, 137, 151, 155, 157, 161, 162, 165, 168, 192

Record Societies, 55, 56, 75, 112, 113, 141, 151

Rectories (Houses). *See* Parsonages

Rectors, 38, 180, 188

Rectors, Institutional, 38

Rectors, Lay, 39

Recusants, 121, 124, 125

Reformation, 6, 29, 33, 43, 99, 119, 127, 128

Registrar General, 74

Registrars' Certificates, 81

Registrars, Diocesan, 100, 106, 108, 118, 123, 124, 126, 149

Religious Orders, 48, 53, 92, 153, 172

Religious Preambles, 147

Religious Tract Society, 20, 168

Replications, 126, 128

Resignation Bonds, 181

Resignations (Clergy), 174

Restoration, 12, 15, 17, 23, 68, 110, 120, 183, 186, 187

Roads, 91, 94, 95

Roman Catholics, 1, 11, 16, 17, 21, 34, 71, 110, 113, 172, 200

Rose's Act, 1812, 67, 73

Royal College of Organists, 25

Royal Historical Society, 56

Royal Navy Chaplains, 190, 192

Rural Dean, 36, 127

Sacrament Certificates, 13, 138

Schoolmasters, 109, 135, 136, 179

Schoolmasters' Licences, 107, 120, 131, 135–7, 179

Schools, 20, 24, 27, 37, 111, 136, 137, 154, 155, 159, 162–5, 179, 204

Scribes, 67, 146, 147, 148

Seating Plans, 96, 98, 99

Sentencing, 35, 122, 123, 124, 126, 127, 128

Sequestration (of Clergy), 125

Sermons, 7, 12, 13, 96, 153, 207

Servants, 103, 142, 145

Servants, Domestic, 161

Servants, Parish, 45, 93, 95

Sexual Offences, 46, 106, 110, 116, 120, 123, 127, 128

Share, 47

Significations, 124, 125

Simeon Trustees, 39

Society for the Promotion of Christian Knowledge, 165, 166, 170

Society for the Propagation of the Gospel, 166, 170, 171, 193

Society for the Relief of Poor Clergymen, 166

Society of Friends. *See* Quakers

Society of Genealogists, 54, 58, 75, 87, 88, 204

Society of the Sacred Mission, 177

Solemn League & Covenant, 13, 136, 138, 183

Southern Province, 52, 84, 133, 144

Spanish Armada, 11

State Papers Domestic, 52

Stipendiary Curates Act, 1813, 44, 179

Subscription Books, 183

Subscriptions, Charitable, 92, 155, 160, 161, 165, 169

Subscriptions, Loyalty, 133, 136, 183

Subsidies, Clerical, 184

Sufferings, Quaker, 14

Summary Proceedings, 122, 123

Sunday Schools, 20, 27, 105, 158, 166, 200

Supremacy. Oath of, 125, 136, 183

Surgeons' Licences, 107, 120, 131, 132, 133, 134, 179

Surplice Fees, 40
Surveys and Rentals, 142
Surveys, Parliamentary, 199, 200
Suspension (of Clergy), 125
Taxation on Vital Events, 64, 70, 71, 73
Taxation, Clerical, 174, 183–5
Terriers. *See* Glebe Terriers
Test Act, 1673, 13, 138
Testators, 91, 108, 144–50
Testimonials, 126, 132, 135, 136, 176, 178, 193
Theological Colleges. *See* Colleges, Theological
Tithe Books, 101, 102
Tithe Commissioners, 101
Tithe Commutation, 41, 44, 100
Tithe Commutation Act, 1836, 18, 44, 100, 101
Tithe Disputes, 17, 40, 100, 102, 121, 122, 127, 128, 139
Tithe Farmers, 100, 107
Tithe Files, 101, 102
Tithe Maps and Apportionments, 100–2
Tithe Records, 99, 101, 102
Tithes, 14, 16, 34, 38–40, 44, 99, 100–2, 106, 120, 126, 179, 203
Title (Clerical), 177, 178, 180
Title Deeds, 105, 126, 142, 155, 204
Toleration Act, 1689, 110
Tractarians. *See* Oxford Movement
Transcripts, 54, 55, 58, 60, 62, 63, 75, 76, 78, 88
Transubstantiation, 7, 136
Triers, 186
United Society for the Propagation of the Gospel, 170–1

Universities' Mission to Central Africa, 172
University Education, 16, 43, 174
University Registers, 174, 175
Urbanization, 18, 21, 73, 161, 179
Vacancies, Clerical, 179, 181
Vacancies, Episcopal, 35, 178
Valor Ecclesiasticus, 184, 203
Vergers, 45, 95
Vermin Eradication, 46, 95
Vestries, 23, 37, 45, 46, 95, 96, 201
Vestry Minutes, 46, 95, 96
Vicar General, 35, 82, 84, 117, 133, 138, 139, 140, 180
Vicars, 38, 180, 188
Village Bands, 25
Visitation Queries. *See* Bishops' Queries, Replies to
Visitations, 17, 35, 36, 45, 46, 67, 94, 107–16, 123, 133, 135, 142, 148, 155, 180
Waifs & Strays Society, 166, 167
War Memorials, 87, 90
Waterloo Churches, 22, 143
Websites. *See* Internet
Welfare State, 26
Westcott House, 177
Widows, 144, 145, 148, 149, 160
Wills, 17, 35, 36, 37, 106, 108, 119, 120, 124, 142, 144–52
Wills, Nuncupative, 146
Wiltshire Record Society, 67
Women, 47, 135, 153, 157, 162, 172
Women, Married, 145
Women's Library, 161
World War I, 26, 168, 189, 190
World Wars, 157